Editors
Gillian Eve Makepeace, M.S.
Sara Connolly

Illustrator
Clint McKnight

Cover Artist
Brenda DiAntonis

Editor In Chief
Ina Massler Levin, M.A.

Creative Director
Karen J. Goldfluss, M.S. Ed.

Art Production Manager
Kevin Barnes

Art Coordinator
Renée Christine Yates

Imaging
Nathan P. Rivera
Ariyanna Simien

Publisher
Mary D. Smith, M.S. Ed.

Author
Melissa Hart, M.F.A.

Teacher Created Resources, Inc.
6421 Industry Way
Westminster, CA 92683
www.teachercreated.com

ISBN: 978-1-4206-2780-0

© *2008 Teacher Created Resources, Inc.*
Made in U.S.A.

Table of Contents

Table of Contents *(cont.)*

Foreword

At its core, this book teaches children and young people how to think critically about media messages, particularly visual media messages.

As the author points out, we are subjected to thousands of mediated images each day. They flash by us so fast that we have no time to think about them. Indeed most are designed to by-pass critical thought. They are carefully crafted to be felt. They tap into our emotions—fear, insecurity, sentimentality, prejudices. Often they purport to portray reality so that, with time, we unquestioningly treat them as being true, and we shape our behavior accordingly, divorced from the world around us.

Nowhere in our formal education have we been taught how to assess and critique these messages and so we have been buffeted by their impact, whether in the purchase of unneeded products, in how we perceive our abilities, or in the way we vote on Election Day. Media education, on the other hand, helps students become smarter in all aspects of their lives.

This book, with its fascinating and fun exercises, is intended to prepare children, a new generation, to see—literally—media images differently, critically. Once given the tools to analyze and think about what they see, children are astonishingly perceptive.

Students are shown how to put their newly acquired skills and insights to use. The skills learned here (and as presented, they are fun to learn) will carry over into other disciplines. Critical thinking about media statistics connects with math. Realizing the role of media-caused anxiety tells us much about psychology and even politics. Analyzing how stories are compellingly told on the screen teaches about clear, vivid writing. The list goes on and on.

More than learning how to make thoughtful, informed decisions and to shape a new, questioning relationship with media, young people also learn how to transform their lives. They perceive themselves differently and more positively. They soon learn that media literacy skills can be applied to all aspects of life.

Young people are great teachers. The great hope is that they will share their new knowledge with their parents and other adults so that, as a society, we all will become more aware and media literate.

Over the years, the media, which have such great potential to perform good, have done greater and greater harm. We have seen an exponential growth in irresponsible content—more violence, more commercialism, more sexualization, more fear-mongering and more deception. Public service has become a rarity. The one sure way to reverse the trend is for audiences to become media literate—for them to recognize the personal and societal consequences of irresponsible media messages and media consumption.

If audiences find such messages unfit for consumption and reject them, media decision-makers must change the media. Indeed, a media-literate public, armed with the tools taught in this text and elsewhere, has the power to force media to redeem themselves and fulfill their great potential and promise.

—Rick Seifert and Rebecca Woolington
MediaThink

How to Use this Book

Media surrounds us, from the moment we wake up in the morning until we go to bed at night. *Media Literacy, Grades 7–8* gives students the opportunity to study most forms of media to which they are exposed almost every day. Each assignment conforms to one or more of the McRel standards for grades 7–8, as noted on pages 6 and 7.

The book begins with a general discussion of media literacy, the various forms of media and how consumers are exposed to it. Students are asked to chart their own media consumption and to examine several forms of media for healthy and unhealthy messages including propaganda and stereotypes.

Historical overviews of each media genre preface each section of the book. This allows students to understand how a particular genre has changed over time, or has given way to a new form of media. Photographs from the National Archives and the Library of Congress offer students the opportunity to view and analyze examples of media from the past and compare them to contemporary media.

Image courtesy of The National Archives (533225)

In each section of the book, students are asked to deconstruct media in a variety of ways; through multiple choice questions, matching exercises, compositions, reviews, and charts. Many assignments require research with the use of books, encyclopedias, and/or the Internet. Each section concludes by offering students the opportunity to create a tangible example of the media genre they have studied. These hands-on projects can be completed alone or in small groups. They offer numerous opportunities for group discussion, and for demonstration among students and parents.

A final project allows students to choose a favorite form of media and create an example. Later, they are asked to deconstruct what they have created to demonstrate a working knowledge of media literacy. A certificate on page 131 of the book can be reproduced and passed out to students as an acknowledgement of completing the activities in this book.

We hope that *Media Literacy, Grades 7–8* will become a valuable addition to your classroom and your curriculum.

Standards

Introduction

Each lesson *in Media Literacy, Grades 7–8*, meets one or more of the following standards, which are used with permission from McREL (Copyright 2007, McREL, Mid-continent Research for Education and Learning. Telephone: 303/337-0990. Website: www.mcrel.org/standards-benchmarks/)

Standard	Page
Uses the general skills and strategies of the writing process	14, 80, 87, 110, 116, 130
Uses the stylistic and rhetorical aspects of writing	26, 49, 54, 60, 74, 87, 99, 110, 116, 130
Uses grammatical and mechanical conventions in written compositions	33, 57, 80, 87, 110, 116, 130
Gathers and uses information for research purposes	15–17, 61, 64, 65, 71, 76, 77, 87, 90, 92, 93, 102, 111, 126, 127
Uses the general skills and strategies of the reading process	46, 47, 48, 49, 53, 54, 81, 128
Uses reading skills and strategies to understand and interpret a variety of informational texts	12, 13, 38, 53, 83, 84, 97, 98–101, 107, 108, 109, 112, 126, 127
Uses listening and speaking strategies for different purposes	46, 47, 48, 49, 53, 54, 81, 128
Uses viewing skills and strategies to understand and interpret visual media	18, 19, 24, 25, 27, 28, 29, 57, 58, 59, 62, 63, 72–74, 83, 84, 91–93, 95, 96–103, 114–115, 125, 126, 127
Understands the characteristics and components of the media	all pages
Understands connections among the various art forms and other disciplines	72, 73, 114, 121–123
Understands that group and cultural influences contribute to human development, identity, and behavior	66, 70, 78, 81, 97, 98–102, 112, 125
Knows environmental and external factors that affect individual/community health	19, 20, 62, 63, 78, 79, 91, 94, 101–102, 124–133
Knows how to maintain mental and emotional health	66-68, 78, 79
Understands and knows how to analyze chronological relationships and patterns	50, 51, 52, 70

Standard	Page
Understands the historical perspective	52, 75, 124–130
Understands the relationship between music and history and culture	47, 48, 60, 75, 124–129
Understands the relationships among science, technology, society, and the individual	49, 75, 12–132
Understands the nature and uses of different forms of technology	42, 43, 44, 45, 59, 75, 127–132
Understands and applies the basic principles of presenting an argument	81
Understands and applies basic principles of logic and reasoning	23, 69, 81, 87, 99
Effectively uses mental processes that are based on identifying similarities and differences	34, 42, 43, 81, 86, 87, 121, 122
Applies decision-making techniques	94
Understands and applies media, techniques, and processes related to the visual arts	36, 44, 88, 103, 123
Knows a range of subject matter, symbols, and potential ideas in the visual arts	72, 73, 76, 77, 82, 83, 84, 85, 95, 97, 100, 104, 107, 108, 114–123
Understands the visual arts in relation to history and cultures	24, 25, 56, 59, 72, 73, 82, 96, 97, 98, 114–121
Contributes to the overall effort of a group	36, 44, 49, 54, 60, 74, 88, 103, 123, 129

What Is Media Literacy?

Each morning, you wake up and get ready for the day. Maybe you listen to the radio or watch a little television. Maybe you glance at the newspaper, or flip through a magazine. You may even play a few minutes of a videogame or surf the Internet.

Outside, you may walk past billboards or ride a bus with ads above the seats. You may decide to see a movie or listen to a good band. You may study a piece of art, or shop for a favorite item.

Each day, you see and hear dozens of forms of media.

The word **media** refers to all the different ways in which people communicate. Each of the examples above represents a type of media.

The word **literacy** means education. Someone who is **media literate** understands how people create media, and how this media affects others.

By the end of this book, you will understand:
- why so many snacks come in red packages.
- why sometimes, you can spot your favorite soda in a movie.
- why people in magazine ads are very attractive.
- why newspapers from three different countries tell the same story in three different ways.
- how people who make commercials get you to buy their products.
- why you believe you need that new videogame.
- what you don't even know you're seeing as you surf the Internet.

Prepare to be amazed as you enter the amazing world of media!

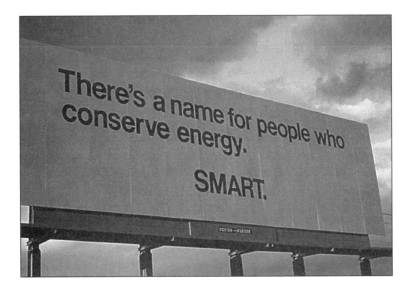

Image courtesy of The National Archives (555380)

Forms of Media

The average person sees and hears hundreds of advertisements a day from media sources all around them. This media directly affects our perception of life. Some sources of media, and their effects, are well known. Here are some examples.

- A 13 year-old boy sees an advertisement on a billboard for a red sports car speeding around a curve on a mountain road. He feels that if he buys the car, he will live an adventurous and exciting life.

- A young woman hears the same song over and over on the radio. She buys the song online and learns the lyrics, feeling that if she knows such a popular song, people will see her as popular, too.

- Two seventh-graders see a movie in which the main character uses a particular type of computer program to design an airplane. They immediately go to their parents and ask if they can buy this program, sure that with it, they'll be able to design airplanes, too.

Other sources of media, and their effects, may surprise you! Here are some examples.

- An eighth-grader goes to the local art museum and studies a painting of a beautiful and graceful ballet dancer in a pink tutu. The student enrolls in dance lessons, believing that if she learns ballet, she will be beautiful and graceful.

- A young man goes to his favorite homepage on the Internet and reads the news. Without thinking about it, he notes an ad for a popular brand of ice cream. When he logs off his computer, he goes to the store and buys a gallon of the ice cream mentioned in the ad.

Here are some of the most common forms of media.

• radio	• billboards	• radio
• websites	• books	• paintings
• movies	• magazines	• e-mail
• television	• print ads	• sculptures
• newspapers	• photographs	• videogames
• mail	• speeches	• packaging

How Much Media?

Directions: Complete the activities 1–3 below.

1. Study the list on the previous page. Then, write down all the forms of media you are exposed to each day.

   _____

   _____

   _____

   _____

2. Now, complete the chart below to show how many hours each day you use each form of media.

Type of Media	Hours Per Day Used
Example: television	two hours
Example: magazine	about 30 minutes

3. Finally, study your completed chart. On the lines below, record your observations about your own media exposure. Explain anything that surprised you.

   _____

   _____

   _____

   _____

   _____

   _____

How Media Affects You

As you have seen from the previous page, media is all around you. It affects how you view yourself and your life. It shapes the choices you make, whether you listen to a particular song, buy a certain brand of shoes, or choose a movie to watch.

Media creators know this. They understand that if they put a beautiful girl in a newspaper ad for a certain cell phone, many people will want to buy that cell phone. They know that when they put particular songs in a popular movie, audiences will leave the theater wanting to buy that music.

Your favorite form of media makes you feel a certain way and it affects your life in a particular manner. For instance, a boy who plays a space-themed videogame may feel excited and happy when he earns a high score. He may feel his heart racing, and his adrenaline pumping as he plays this game. He might find that he rushes through homework and chores so that he can get more time to play his favorite game, or that his play has inspired him to study to be an astronaut!

Directions: Think about the media that you see every day and then answer the questions below.

1. On the line below, write down the form of media that is most important to you. Refer to the list you made on page 10.

   _____

2. Now, explain how this form of media makes you feel, and how it affects your life.

   _____

   _____

   _____

   _____

   _____

   _____

   _____

   _____

   _____

   _____

   _____

   _____

   _____

   _____

   _____

Deconstructing Media

The creators of media know how to shape your interests and desires through the use of images and sounds. To be truly media literate, you must be aware of these persuasive advertising techniques.

If you wanted to understand how a leaf is created, you would look at it under a magnifying glass, or even a microscope, and break it down into parts to be studied.

Likewise, if you wanted to be a professional golfer, you would listen closely to your coach and break down your swing into small actions—perfecting each until you understood exactly how to drive a ball.

This breaking down of a large object or action into pieces is called **deconstruction**.

You need to be able to deconstruct media in its various forms. As you view or listen to a particular type of media, ask yourself the questions below. Example answers have been given for this poster.

Image courtesy of the Library of Congress
(LC-USZC4-12098)

Question	Example Answer
Who paid for this media?	A French bicycle company trying to advertise and sell its product.
To what age group, economic group, and gender does this media appeal?	Young women from any economic background.
What text or images bring you to this conclusion?	A lady is featured in the ad; she seems quite young and free.
What kind of lifestyle is presented? How is it glamorized?	A great lifestyle where you'll be glamorous, patriotic, and pretty.
What is the obvious message in this media?	You should buy the bicycle.
What are the hidden messages in this media?	If you buy this bicycle you will be pretty, glamorous, and happy.
In what ways is this a healthy or unhealthy example of media?	Bicycling is healthy, but riding without a helmet is not.

Persuasive Techniques

Directions: This page lists persuasive advertising techniques and how they are used. Study the list and think of ads you have seen that use this technique.

Technique	Example
Symbols—these are words, places, images, songs, etc., that represent something else.	A white dove traditionally symbolizes peace.
Hyperbole—this is another word for exaggeration.	Our hot dogs are the tastiest in the world!
Fear—sometimes, media makes us afraid that if we don't pay attention, something bad could happen.	Buy this car alarm, or your convertible will be stolen!
Humor—making someone laugh is a particularly effective persuasive technique.	This commercial with dancing dogs is so funny that I want to buy the dog food being advertised!
The Big Lie—believe it or not, sometimes creators of media don't tell the truth.	Sugar-Crunch Cereal offers you a nutritional way to start your day.
Testimonials—using famous people to sell products and ideas.	These World Series winners chew a particular brand of gum, so I should, too!
Repetition—hearing or seeing something over and over makes a product stick in your head so you remember the brand or product.	You should shop at Joe's Clothes because Joe's Clothes gives you the best deals on quality items that you can only find at Joe's Clothes.
Name Calling—characters make fun of other characters in order to sell something.	That new kid is odd because he doesn't eat a certain type of candy bar.
Flattery—if you compliment someone, he or she will pay attention.	You're so cool and smart for eating that type of candy bar!
Bribery—this offers something we want.	Buy one, get one free.
Bandwagon—this technique implies that everyone else is involved, so why aren't you?	All the popular kids wear this brand of jeans. Shouldn't you?
Warm and Fuzzy—cute, sweet images sell products and ideas.	Those cute cats love that brand of fabric softener, and so will I.
Beautiful People—good-looking models make us believe we can look like them.	I'll look just like her if I wear this type of lip gloss.
Plain Folks—people just like us use the same product.	That guy with the chewing gum looks like me, so I should buy this chewing gum.
Scientific Evidence—statistics and charts persuade us that something is worthwhile.	Nine out of 10 teachers surveyed say that children should get at least eight hours of sleep a night if they are going to do well in school.

Persuasion in Action

A **slogan** is a line used by the media to advertise a particular product or action. You can analyze a slogan for specific persuasive advertising techniques. Here are two examples.

"Strut like a star in Red Carpet Shoes for Her."

This slogan implies that stars on the red carpet buy and wear these shoes and these people tend to be thought of as beautiful and attractive.

"STOP AND LOOK BOTH WAYS . . . FOR LIFE."

This slogan uses fear—if you don't look both ways, you might get killed!

Directions: Identify a slogan from a magazine, newspaper, television, or radio commercial. Write the slogan below then list the persuasive advertising techniques that are used.

A **jingle** is a short, catchy song used by the media to advertise a particular product or action. Like a slogan, jingles contain persuasive advertising techniques. Here is an example.

"IF YOU LIKE CLEAN AIR,
SAFE FOR YOU AND ME,
SHOW THE WORLD YOU CARE—
STOP AND PLANT A TREE!"

The persuasive advertising techniques for this jingle are symbols (a tree is a symbol for clean air), fear (if you don't plant a tree, our air will be dirty), bandwagon (show everyone that you care), and bribery (if you plant a tree, we'll have clean air).

Directions: Below, write down one jingle from the media then list the persuasive advertising techniques that are used.

_____

_____

_____

_____

_____

Propaganda

Propaganda is the use of false information to sell products or ideas. It was used most famously in 1898, when newspaper owner William Randolph Hearst asked an artist to provide sketches of Cubans rebelling against Spanish rulers during the Spanish-American War.

The artist wired a message to Hearst explaining that he saw no signs of war. Then, Hearst implied that he would make up details about war in his newspaper. "You provide the pictures," he replied, "and I'll provide the war."

Why would Hearst turn to propaganda? A sensational story sells newspapers!

Propaganda appeared later on recruitment posters for World War I and World War II.

Directions: Study the World War II poster on page 16, then answer these questions.

1. What idea is being sold by this poster?

   _____

   _____

   _____

2. What persuasive advertising technique is used here?

   _____

   _____

   _____

3. What does this poster promise if you save your scrap metal, paper, rubber, and rags?

   _____

   _____

   _____

4. Can you think of any improvements to make the poster even more effective?

   _____

   _____

   _____

   _____

Image courtesy of the Library of Congress (LC-USZC2-5676)

Creating Propaganda

On page 15, you learned that propaganda is the deliberate use of false information to sell products or ideas.

Directions: Study a newspaper or magazine advertisement for an example of propaganda. Sketch a picture of the ad in the box below, then answer questions 1 and 2. Look at number 3, then copy the sentence onto the blank lines, filling in the gaps appropriately for your chosen ad. Read and complete number 4.

1. What product or idea is this advertisement attempting to sell?

   _____

   _____

2. What persuasive advertising technique is used here?

   _____

   _____

3. This advertiser says that if I _____ this product or idea _____ will occur.

   _____

   _____

   _____

4. Finally, create your own advertisement that makes use of propaganda. Choose an idea or product that you wish to sell. On a separate sheet of paper, design an ad in which you demonstrate your understanding of propaganda. Make sure that your advertisement contains a slogan and images that help to reinforce your false information!

Stereotypes

A stereotype is an oversimplified portrayal of someone. "Dumb blond," "insensitive male," and "wicked stepmother" are all examples of a stereotype. Many forms of media use stereotypes. These are an easy way to get a point across quickly. However, stereotypes often end up hurting people.

Directions: Consider the scenarios in the chart below. Each uses a stereotype. Describe who is being stereotyped. Then explain who might be hurt by this media.

Scenario	Who is Being Stereotyped And How?	Who Might be Hurt By This Media?
1. A bookstore films a new TV commercial. In it, Asian people read soberly on benches beside shelves. Anglo and Latino people laugh at tables in the bookstore's café.		
2. A newspaper runs an ad for cell phones. In it, a very thin woman in a tight red dress holds a phone to her ear. Handsome men surround her. In one corner of the ad, a woman of average weight wears overalls and stands alone looking enviously at the woman with the phone.		
3. A children's book has a chapter in which the narrator, living in the 1800s, meets a Native American. The narrator says that the Native American smells bad, wears hardly any clothes, and is ignorant because he can't speak English.		

Stereotypes *(cont.)*

Directions: To better understand stereotypes, create your own. On the left-hand side of the column, create a stereotypical description for the character and form of media mentioned. On the right side, create an original description that is free of stereotypes. The first one has been done for you.

Character	Form of Media	Stereotype	Original
Scientist	Radio ad	This radio ad features a man's voice speaking in a British accent. He uses very big words and speaks in a boring, sing-song voice.	This radio ad features a young woman speaking enthusiastically. She speaks in words that are easy to understand, and she sounds as if she might be from the Southern United States.
Football player	Television commercial		
Teacher	Magazine ad		
Cheerleader	Movie		

Healthy Media?

Healthy media sends positive messages to consumers and doesn't do anything to harm them physically or mentally. One example of healthy media might be a television commercial that notes the importance of exercise by showing a group of children laughing and playing soccer.

Unhealthy media hurts the consumer. Think about a television show in which a group of girls are being mean to another girl because she is wearing a certain brand of jeans. Viewers may end up believing that you'll only be liked if you wear particular clothes. Another example of unhealthy media might be a radio commercial that urges people to spend their money at a casino. If a listener has a gambling problem, and is tempted to visit this location, he or she might be negatively affected.

Directions: Study the examples of media on page 21 and answer these questions.

School Meal Poster

1. What idea does this poster from the mid-1900s try to sell?

   _____

   _____

2. Is this media healthy or unhealthy? Explain your answer.

   _____

   _____

   _____

   _____

Soda Advertisement

1. What product is this ad trying to sell?

   _____

2. What techniques of persuasion does this ad use?

   _____

   _____

3. Is this ad healthy or unhealthy? Explain your answer.

   _____

   _____

   _____

   _____

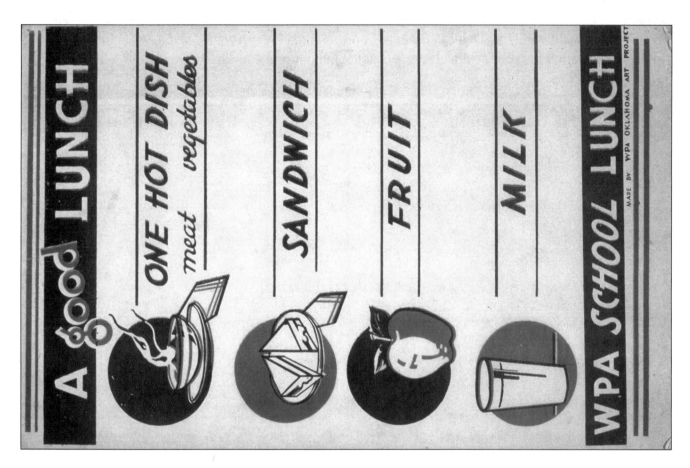

Image courtesy of the Library of Congress (LC-USZC2-5427)

Healthy Media? *(cont.)*

Directions: Now it's your turn. In the spaces below, design one example of healthy media, and one example of unhealthy media. This can be an ad, a poster, or another form of media. Use the lines to write an explanation for your media. If there is not enough room, you can continue your work on the back of the sheet.

Healthy Media	Unhealthy Media

_____

_____

_____

_____

Hidden Messages

Media-literate consumers have the skill to experience a piece of media and tell what messages it brings. These messages are both obvious and hidden. For instance, a print ad for soda might show three beautiful, smiling women sipping glasses of soda at a table while a handsome waiter looks on. The obvious message of this ad is that you should drink this soda. The hidden message of this ad is that if you buy this soda, you will be beautiful and happy and surrounded by good-looking people.

Directions: Read the descriptions of media below. Then, explain the obvious message and the hidden message.

1. In a television commercial, a boy eats a bowl of cereal. Suddenly, he is able to fly over his house and his city with amazing super-powers.

Obvious Message	Hidden Message

2. On a radio show for children, a doctor is the special guest. He tells listeners that it's important to eat fruits and vegetables. "That's what I did," he says, "and now I'm a doctor!"

Obvious Message	Hidden Message

3. On a billboard, there is a photo of a cat with a dead bird in its mouth. Under the picture are the words, "Keep your cat inside because nature is not a snack-bar."

Obvious Message	Hidden Message

First Media

Prehistoric people created their own media to communicate with each other. They designed petroglyphs—drawing or carvings on rocks. Rather than advertising a professionally produced product, they used these petroglyphs to comment on their surroundings, food sources, and weather.

Here is a picture of *Newspaper Rock* located in Southern Utah. Native Americans carved these petroglyphs during prehistoric and historic periods.

Image courtesy of The National Archives (545671)

Directions: Study the picture of Newspaper Rock's petroglyphs. Below, explain what you think the creators of these drawings were communicating.

_____

_____

_____

_____

_____

Understanding Petroglyphs

Directions: Using encyclopedias, books, and the Internet, research petroglyphs. In the space below, sketch one petroglyph that you find particularly interesting. Continue by answering the questions.

1. In what location was this petroglyph found?
   _____

2. Who created this petroglyph? How did you come to this conclusion?
   _____
   _____
   _____

3. What objects can you find in this petroglyph?
   _____
   _____

4. What ideas do you believe are being communicated in this petroglyph?
   _____
   _____

Make Your Own Petroglyph

Directions: Develop symbols and create a petroglyph of your own to send a message to people. Remember—no written words allowed! Find a small rock with one flat side and paint and brushes. Complete steps 1–3 below.

1. Fill out the symbol-chart. In the top row, write the words you will convey with your petroglyph. On the bottom row, draw a symbol for each word. An example is done for you.

Word	Sun							
Symbol	☀							

2. Now, create your petroglyph. Use the paint and brushes to paint your symbols on your rock.

3. When you have finished your petroglyph, display it for others to study. See if they can interpret your symbols correctly. Then, in the space below, write one paragraph explaining what messages you wished to convey with your petroglyph. Use the space at the bottom to write a message.

_____

_____

_____

_____

26

Print Advertisements

Print advertisements are an extremely popular form of media. Most of us rely on sight more than the other senses. For this reason, visual images and text are extremely powerful forms of advertising.

Print advertisements have been around ever since the first printing press turned out newspapers and flyers.

On page 28, there is an example of a print ad from 1926. You can deconstruct it for meaning just as you would analyze any other form of media.

Directions: Study the advertisement on page 28, then answer the questions below.

1. What is this print ad trying to sell?

   _____

2. What is the name of the company that paid for this ad?

   _____

3. This ad likely appealed to what kind of person?

   _____

   _____

4. How does the advertiser try to get people to buy these bats?

   _____

   _____

5. What is the obvious message in this ad?

   _____

   _____

6. After viewing this ad, some people may believe what will happen to them if they buy a Louisville Slugger Bat?

   _____

   _____

   _____

7. Do you think this ad was effective? Explain your answer.

   _____

   _____

   _____

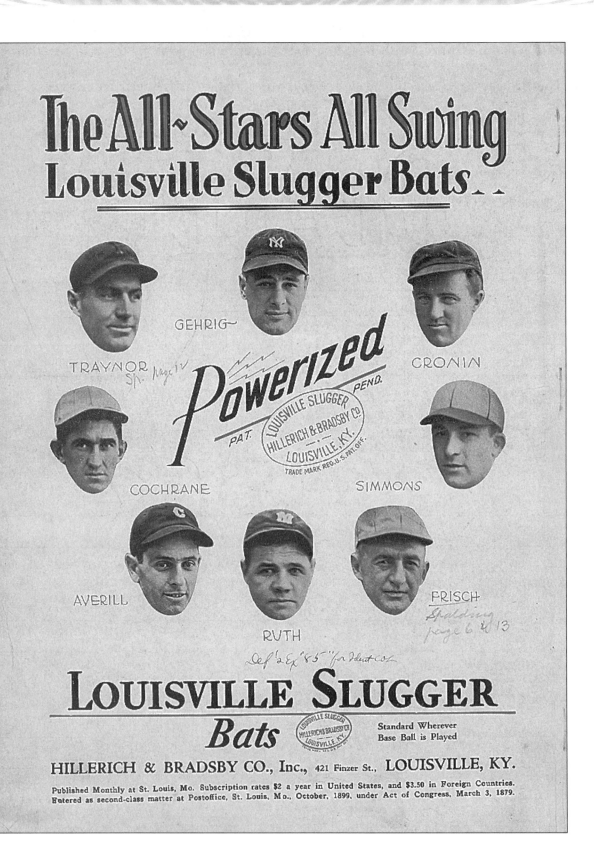

Image courtesy of The National Archives (279238)

Early Print Ads

Directions: Look at the advertisement from 1861 on page 30. Circle the correct letter to complete each sentence below.

1. This advertisement is for
    a. boots.
    b. clothes.
    c. drawing.
    d. pullers.

2. This advertisement was paid for by
    a. For Sale Wholesale.
    b. boot pullers.
    c. The American Boot Puller Company.
    d. gentlemen.

3. This advertisement will appeal mostly to
    a. wealthy young women.
    b. poor bedridden men.
    c. well-off gentlemen.
    d. mothers with sons.

4. The man in the background is an example of
    a. beautiful people.
    b. warm and fuzzy.
    c. hyperbole.
    d. fear.

5. The obvious message in this advertisement is
    a. this boot puller helps you to put on and take off boots.
    b. his boot puller makes people tense.
    c. this boot puller is expensive.
    d. you will be handsome if you use this boot puller.

6. The hidden message in this advertisement is
    a. you do not really need a boot puller.
    b. you will be handsome and graceful if you buy this boot puller.
    c. this boot puller is difficult to use.
    d. using this boot puller will earn you good friends.

Image courtesy of the Library of Congress (LC-USZ62-4627)

Early Print Ads *(cont.)*

On pages 29–30, you studied one example of an early print advertisement. On page 32 is another print ad, created in 1922.

Directions: Deconstruct the print advertisement by answering the questions below.

1. Who paid for this advertisement?

_____

_____

2. What is this advertiser trying to sell?

_____

_____

3. What types of people might you have found in the audience for this film?

_____

_____

4. List three persuasive phrases that advertisers use to get potential consumers' attention.

_____

_____

_____

_____

5. Why might an advertisement like this no longer appear in newspapers today?

_____

_____

_____

_____

THE MOVING PICTURE WORLD

1039

Buffalo   Bill

The last of the great Indian fighters, Colonel Wm. F. Cody and Lieutenant General Nelson A. Miles (retired) of the United States Army, are the leading players in this most realistic film of the age.

This picture, which has been APPROVED BY THE UNITED STATES GOVERNMENT and made under the DIRECTION OF THE WAR DEPARTMENT, has attracted the attention *of the entire world.*

"THE INDIAN WARS"

As a Money-Maker this film is without an equal. The Advertising Possibilities of the picture are unlimited. It is a FIVE-REEL THRILLER THAT WILL LIVE FOREVER.

1000 INDIANS, many of whom were leaders in the original battles; 12th U.S. CAVALRY, and MANY OFFICERS now retired, again took their places in the re-enacted scenes.

Historically Correct and all scenes TAKEN ON THE EXACT LOCATION of the original battles.

State Rights Now Ready   Get Busy!

THE POSTERS will STOP THE CROWDS and get you the business—6 one-sheets, 3 three-sheets, 1 six-sheet, 2 eight-sheets, 2 sixteen-sheets.

EXHIBITORS—Write or wire us at once and if your state has not been sold, we will book you direct.

General Nelson A. Miles (U. S. A. Retired)

THE COL. WM. F. CODY (BUFFALO BILL) HISTORICAL PICTURE CO.

521 First National Bank Bldg.
CHICAGO   ILL.

An American Aborigine

Image courtesy of The National Archives (292756)

Contemporary Print Ads

You can see from studying the print ads on pages 27–32 that advertising has changed quite a bit over the centuries.

Directions: Find a print advertisement in a contemporary magazine or newspaper. Cut it out and paste it onto a separate sheet of paper. Alternatively, you may choose to sketch the advertisement. Then, study the ad and deconstruct it in a short essay on the lines below. In your essay, make sure you include the following points.

- who paid for the advertisement
- the age group, economic group, and gender to which the ad appeals
- the text and images that brought you to the above conclusion
- techniques of persuasion used in the ad
- the lifestyle presented and how it is glamorized
- obvious and hidden messages
- how the advertisement is healthy or unhealthy

_____

_____

_____

_____

_____

_____

_____

_____

_____

_____

_____

_____

_____

_____

_____

_____

_____

_____

Compare and Contrast

Print advertisements have changed a great deal over time. Images are different, as are language, messages, and techniques of persuasion. You can study how print ads have changed by comparing an early ad with another that has appeared recently in print.

Directions: Using books, encyclopedias, and the Internet, locate an early print advertisement. Possible search engine words include *early print advertisements*, *historical advertisements*, and *pictorial Americana*. Sketch the ad you choose in the first space below. Then, locate a contemporary print ad in a magazine or newspaper. Sketch this ad in the second space below.

Using the Venn diagram on page 35, compare and contrast the two print advertisements. In the circle on the left, write features of the early print ad. In the circle on the right, write features of the contemporary print ad. Where the two circles overlap, write features that are common to both ads. Make sure you look at similarities and differences in text, images, and persuasion techniques. Finally, write a paragraph, including specific examples, of how you think print advertisements have changed over the last 150 years.

Directions: Use this Venn diagram to compare and contrast your two chosen print advertisements. In the circle on the left, write features of the early print ad. In the circle on the right, features of the contemporary print ad. Where the two circles overlap, write features that are common to both ads.

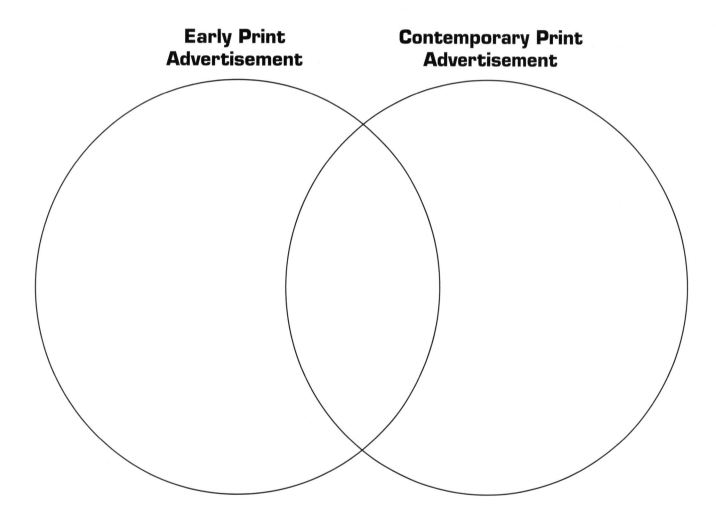

Early Print Advertisement

Contemporary Print Advertisement

Create Your Own Print Ad

Now it's your turn to demonstrate all that you have learned about print advertising.

Directions: On a separate sheet of paper, design your own print ad for a product of your choice. Once complete, answer these questions to deconstruct your ad.

1. What product is being advertised?

   _____

2. To what age group, economic group, and gender does your print advertisement appeal?

   _____

   _____

3. What techniques of persuasion do you use in your ad?

   _____

   _____

4. What are the obvious messages in your ad?

   _____

   _____

5. What are the hidden messages, if any?

   _____

   _____

6. What kind of lifestyle is being presented? How is it glamorized (if applicable)?

   _____

   _____

7. How is your ad an example of healthy or unhealthy media?

   _____

   _____

   _____

Billboards

Billboards are print advertisements on a grand scale. In 1835, a man named Jared Bell printed enormous posters, also called *bills*, to advertise a circus. He placed them outside, and introduced a new form of media! By 1867, advertisers leased space on the sides of buildings and on fences for their enormous ads. Now you can see billboards advertising everything from food to fairs to energy conservation!

This is an example of a circus bill from 1840.

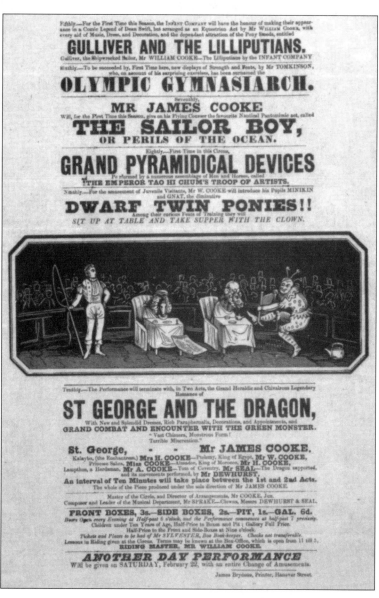

Image courtesy of the Library of Congress, Prints and Photographs Division (LC-USZC4-6889)

Early Billboards

Directions: Study the billboard and then deconstruct it by matching the correct letter to the correct number.

Image courtesy of the Library of Congress, Prints and Photographs Division (LC-USZ62-91461)

1. product   **a.** If you live in America, you will be happy.

2. consumer   **b.** America has the world's highest standard of living

3. slogan   **c.** bandwagon

4. persuasive technique   **d.** Americans

5. obvious message   **e.** "There's no way like the American way."

6. hidden message   **f.** American way of life

Early Billboards (cont.)

Some billboards are political. The one below, created in 1948, is a campaign billboard.

Directions: Study the billboard and then deconstruct it by answering the questions.

Image courtesy of The National Archives (187021)

1. What political position did Gerald Ford, Jr. hope to achieve with this billboard?

   _____

2. Describe the appearance of Ford in the ad. Why is he portrayed in this manner?

   _____

   _____

   _____

3. To what type of person would this billboard appeal?

   _____

   _____

4. Who is the "you" in the slogan, "to work for you in Congress"?

   _____

   _____

5. Why do you think there is a circle of stars in the upper left corner of this billboard?

   _____

   _____

Today's Billboards

What billboards do you see every day in your city or town? Do you pass by without noticing them, or do you enjoy looking at them?

Directions: Choose two interesting billboards from your location. Sketch them in the spaces below, and then complete the chart on page 41 for each billboard.

Today's Billboards *(cont.)*

Directions: Complete the chart below taking information from your two chosen billboards.

Question	Billboard One	Billboard Two
Who paid for this billboard?		
To what age group, economic group, and gender does this billboard appeal?		
What text or images bring you to the conclusion above?		
What techniques of persuasion are used?		
What kind of lifestyle is presented? How is it glamorized?		
What is the obvious message on this billboard?		
What are the hidden messages on this billboard?		

Compare and Contrast

Now that you've studied billboards from the past and present, consider how this form of media has changed over the years.

Directions: Using encyclopedias, books, and the Internet, locate a billboard created before 1970. Possible search engine words include *history of billboards*, *billboard advertising*, and *early billboards*. Sketch your chosen billboard in the space below. Then, choose one of the contemporary local billboards you sketched on page 40 and complete the Venn diagram on page 43 comparing the two billboards. In the square on the left, write features of the pre-1970s billboard. In the square on the right, write features of the contemporary billboard. Where the two squares overlap, write features that are common to both billboards.

Make sure you look at similarities and differences in text, images, and persuasion techniques. Finally, on a separate piece of paper, write a paragraph, including specific examples of how you think billboards have changed over the years.

Compare and Contrast *(cont.)*

Directions: Use this Venn diagram to compare and contrast your two chosen billboards. In the square on the left, write features of the pre-1970s billboard. In the square on the right, write features of the contemporary billboard. Where the two squares overlap, write features that are common to both billboards.

Pre-1970s Billboard

Contemporary Billboard

Create a Billboard

Using what you've learned about billboards as a form of media, create your own billboard by following the directions below. You will need two-to-three pieces of scrap paper; butcher paper (two sheets six feet long); transparent tape (one piece six feet long); pencils with erasers; markers or paint and brushes.

Directions: Get into groups of three or four. Discuss what your billboard will advertise. On the scrap paper, sketch a quick design.

Lay out the pieces of butcher paper on the floor parallel to each other. Tape them together at their longest end, forming a large rectangle. You may leave the paper on the floor or tape it to a wall. Sketch the design for your billboard on the butcher paper. Make sure to include both images and text. Use markers or paint and brushes to add color to your billboard. Let it dry, and then display it in your hallway or in your room.

Finally, answer these questions to explain your billboard.

1. What techniques of persuasion did you use?

   _____

   _____

2. What is the obvious message of your billboard?

   _____

   _____

3. What is the hidden message of your billboard, if any?

   _____

   _____

4. How is your billboard an example of healthy or unhealthy media?

   _____

   _____

   _____

   _____

Radio

Radio broadcasts have been around since the early part of the 20th century. Here are a few highlights from the history of this exciting form of media.

1887——————→	Scientist Heinrich Hertz first detected radio waves.
1894——————→	Inventor Guglielmo Marconi invented a spark transmitter with an antenna. He formed the Wireless Telegraph and Signal Company when he was 23 years old!
1918——————→	Political broadcasts began to air.
1919——————→	David Sarnoff became General Manager of the Radio Corporation of America (RCA) in 1919 and sought mass production of radio music boxes.
1920——————→	Westinghouse Vice President Harry Davis and engineer Frank Conrad created a 100-watt transmitter in Pittsburgh, PA. KDKA began regularly scheduled broadcasts every evening from 8:30–9:30 P.M.
1922——————→	The *broadcasting boom!* Over 500 stations started broadcasting by the end of this year.

Image courtesy of the Library of Congress, Prints and Photographs Division (LC-USZ62-132498)

This photograph is from 1940 and it shows New York Mayor Fiorello La Guardia delivering a message at the WNYC public radio station.

Radio Ad Techniques

Radio advertisers are called *sponsors*. They help to pay for programs on the radio. In return, they get to advertise their product.

Advertising on the radio requires different techniques than those used in print advertising. Listeners are unable to see beautiful people selling toothpaste and hair conditioner. They can't observe a child enjoying a bowl of delicious granola. So what is a sponsor to do?

Directions: Fill out the chart with suggestions for how the producer of a radio commercial might use sound to get across persuasive advertising techniques. The first square of the chart has been done for you.

Persuasive Advertising Technique	How to Convey it on the Radio
Beautiful people	Have people speak in sultry, cultured voices, possibly with British accents.
Bandwagon	
Fear	
Warm and fuzzy	
Symbols	
Humor	
Testimonial	
Repetition	
Scientific evidence	

Historic Radio Ads

The Internet allows you to listen to all sorts of radio commercials from the last century.

Directions: Using an Internet search engine, identify two radio commercials. Type these key words into your search engine: *old radio commercials*, *historic radio commercials*, and *radio commercials from the 1930s, 1940s, 1950s* and see what you find! Then, deconstruct each commercial by completing the table below.

Question	Commercial One	Commercial Two
What is this radio commercial advertising?		
Which sponsors paid for this radio commercial?		
To what listeners would this radio commercial appeal?		
In this radio commercial, how is sound used as a persuasive technique?		
What is the obvious message of this radio commercial?		
What is the hidden message of this radio commercial?		
Is this radio commercial healthy or unhealthy? How did you come to this conclusion?		

Contemporary Radio Ads

How have radio advertisements changed over the years? Have they become more or less sophisticated? Shorter or longer? More or less entertaining?

Directions: Listen to two contemporary commercials on the radio, and, if possible, record a few so you can listen multiple times. Jot down notes about each commercial as you listen—you may need to listen more than once. Using your notes, write a short essay deconstructing each commercial. Use the questions below to ensure you cover all the points.

Questions to consider

- What product or idea is this radio commercial advertising?
- Who paid for this radio commercial?
- To what age group, economic group, and gender does this commercial appeal?
- What techniques of persuasion are used in this commercial?
- What kind of lifestyle is presented? How is it glamorized?
- What is the obvious message in this commercial?
- What are the hidden messages in this commercial?
- In what ways is this commercial a healthy or unhealthy example of media?

Essay

_____

_____

_____

_____

_____

_____

_____

_____

_____

_____

_____

Your Radio Commercial

Now it's your turn to write and produce a radio commercial! You will need lined paper, pen or pencil, and a tape recorder or computer with recording capability.

Directions: In groups of two-to-four, choose a product or idea to advertise. Decide how long to make your radio commercial. Typically, radio ads are short; they range from 15– to 30– to 60–second spots.

Write a script for your commercial and decide who will voice each part. If you need sound effects, obtain these. Practice the commercial multiple times and adjust as needed. Record your commercial— you may need to record several takes.

Once it is complete and you are happy as a group with the commercial, deconstruct it in one paragraph. Be sure to explain the following:

- your product
- techniques of persuasion
- obvious messages
- healthy or unhealthy media

- your target audience
- type of lifestyle
- hidden messages

_____

_____

_____

_____

_____

_____

_____

_____

_____

_____

_____

_____

_____

_____

Finally, play your radio commercial to the rest of your class.

The First Radio Shows

Long before the Internet, before movies and television and videogames, people listened to the radio for fun. Families crowded around the radio after dinner each night to hear Westerns such as "Hopalong Cassidy," mysteries such as "Cloak and Dagger," and comedies like "Amos and Andy."

Many libraries carry copies of these old radio shows. The Internet allows you to listen to hundreds of these as well.

Directions: Check out copies of radio shows from the library, or, using an Internet search engine, find two radio shows from before the 1950s. Type these key words into your search engine: *old time radio show*, *old radio*, and *radio lovers*.

Then, deconstruct each radio show by filling in the blank spots in the dialogue below and on page 51.

Radio Show One

Jess: Sam, what are you listening to?

Sam: Oh, it's an old radio show called _____.

Jess: What's it about?

Sam: It's about _____

_____

_____.

Jess: Sounds interesting. What kind of people listen to this show, anyhow?

Sam: Mostly people who are _____

_____.

Jess: How does this radio show use sound?

Sam: Well, there are sound effects like _____

_____.

Jess: I'm just curious, what messages do you get from this show?

Sam: The obvious message of this particular show is _____

_____

_____.

Directions: Again, deconstruct the second radio show by filling in the blank spots in the dialogue below.

Radio Show Two

Pat: You sure are enjoying that radio show. What's it called?

Kyle: The name of it is _____.

Pat: Do you think it's healthy to be listening to a show like that?

Kyle: Well, the way I see it, _____

_____

_____.

Pat: Aren't there all sorts of hidden messages in this show?

Kyle: The only hidden messages I find are _____

_____

_____.

Pat: I see. What sponsors pay for this show, anyhow?

Kyle: I have heard ads for _____

_____.

Pat: This show is awfully loud. How does it use sound to create emotion?

Kyle: Oh, it's fascinating. To create a sense of _____, the show uses _____

_____.

And to create a sense of _____, it uses _____

_____.

Pat: Fascinating. So how old are typical listeners, and do you think they're male or female, or both?

Kyle: I would guess that listeners are _____

_____.

War of the Worlds

In 1938, a young actor and director by the name of Orson Welles broadcast a piece on the radio that caused people great fear, and later, great shame.

On the day before Halloween, Welles read a play adapted from H.G. Wells' famous science fiction novel called *The War of the Worlds*. It was a book about Martians invading Earth. Welles read one section which sounded like a news broadcast reporting the Martian invasion.

The play was so convincing that listeners believed their planet really was being invaded by Mars. Cars jammed the roads as people tried to escape. Other listeners hid in cellars. Some wrapped wet towels around their heads, hoping to avoid the Martians' poison gas.

Directions: Welles' radio show caused a national panic. You can listen to it on tapes from your local library. Alternatively, you can listen or read a transcript of the show on the Internet. Type the following words into a search engine: *War of the Worlds radio*, or *Orson Welles radio*, to find an appropriate link. Listen to part of the broadcast. Then, fill in the chart below. The relevant part of this broadcast occurs within the first five minutes.

1. Briefly describe what is going on in this story.	
2. What details in this radio show made people really believe that Martians were invading Earth?	
3. Do you believe that the same panic could happen today because of a radio show? Explain your answer.	

Children's Radio Shows

Radio shows for children have been around for years and years. In the 1930s and 1940s, they lasted between 15 and 30 minutes and always ended with a cliffhanger, that is a conclusion that left the hero in trouble. This would make kids tune in the next day to find out what happened to the Green Hornet, or Popeye the Sailor, or Chick Carter—Boy Detective.

These days, radio shows for kids still exist on many radio stations around the world. In addition, children can now listen to podcasts created just for young people. A podcast is a digital media file that you can download and play on your computer or other listening device.

Directions: Using a radio or the Internet, listen to two radio programs for young people. Then, answer the questions below to deconstruct each program.

Most local radio stations have websites with program schedules. To locate children's radio shows on the Internet, type the following words into a search engine: *children's radio shows*, *children's podcasts*, or *radio for kids*.

Question	Radio Program One	Radio Program Two
To what age group, economic group, and gender does this radio show appeal?		
What sounds bring you to the conclusion above?		
What kind of lifestyle is presented? How is it glamorized?		
What is the obvious message in this radio show?		
What are the hidden messages in this radio show?		
Who sponsored this radio show—that is, what commercials did you hear?		
In what ways is this radio show a healthy and/or unhealthy example of media?		

Create Your Radio Show

You can write and record a five- to ten-minute radio show just as you've been studying in this book. You will need several sheets of lined paper, a pen or pencil, a tape recorder or computer with recording capability, and materials to use for sound effects.

Directions: In a group of three-to-four, decide what format your radio show will take. Will you teach kids how to do something on your show, like whistling or juggling? Will you interview guests like a professional squirrel trainer or a favorite teacher? What commercials will you have on your show?

Write a script for your radio show. Decide who will play which part. To see a proper format, type the words *radio script* into your favorite Internet search engine.

Think about any sound effects you will need. Obtain materials as needed to create these sounds then record your radio show. You may need to record several takes.

Now deconstruct your commercial by filling in the chart below.

Audience?	
Product or Idea You're Selling?	
Lifestyle Presented?	
How Do You Use Sound?	
Obvious Messages?	
Hidden Messages?	
Healthy or Unhealthy?	

Finally, play your radio commercial for your class!

54

Television

Television programming has a long and interesting history. Here are some of the highlights.

1862	The first still image is transferred over wires.
1876	The term *cathode rays* is coined to describe the light emitted when an electric current is forced through a vacuum tube.
1884	Images are sent over wires using a rotating metal disk with 18 lines of resolution.
1924/25	Inventors sent mechanical transmissions of images over wire circuits.
1927	Bell Telephone and the U.S. Department of Commerce conduct the first long-distance use of television between Washington D.C. and New York City.
1929	The first television studio opened.
1936	About 200 television sets are in use across the world.
1939	The New York World's Fair demonstrates television and receivers. Some had to be coupled with a radio for sound.
1948	One million homes in the United States have television sets.
1956	The first remote control, called the Zenith Space Commander, is introduced.
1966	The first satellite carries television broadcasts internationally.
1967	Most television broadcasts are in color.
1969	600 million people watch the first television transmission from the moon.

Television Commercials

Television commercials have both entertained and annoyed viewers since 1941. On July 1 of that year, the Federal Communications Commission allowed commercials to be aired on TV for the first time ever.

NBC aired a 10-second commercial to advertise wristwatches. The Bulova Watch Company paid the network seven dollars for this commercial. Seeing that a profit could be made, other stations began showing commercials as well.

In 1952, a television commercial advertised Mr. Potato Head®. The toy grossed $4 million in the first year of production. The success of this ad gave businesses a taste of just how powerful a commercial could be!

Many commercials rely on a jingle—a catchy song that sticks in the viewer's head long after the commercial is over. Some use animation to sell a product or idea. Some businesses create a recognizable character that stars in different commercials year after year.

These days, researchers estimate that people watch about 40,000 television commercials a year. This form of media is seen as the most valuable form of mass-market advertising.

Classic TV Commercials

Television commercials have changed quite a bit over the decades. In the beginning, a television show might have just one commercial that lasted a minute and a half. That's quite long compared to the 15- or 30-second commercials we see today.

Directions: Using the Internet, view two commercials that aired in the 1950s, 1960s, or 1970s. Type the words *classic commercials*, *old commercials*, or *television commercials* into your favorite search engine. Deconstruct each commercial in a short paragraph, below. Ask your teacher for two copies of this sheet or write your paragraphs on a separate piece of paper. In each paragraph, make sure you look at the following points:

- Who paid for this commercial?
- To what group does it appeal?
- What techniques of persuasion are used?
- What kind of lifestyle is presented?
- What hidden and obvious messages exist?
- How is this commercial healthy or unhealthy media?

In your paragraphs, also describe what you noticed about these classic commercials—what is interesting about them? What do you like? What do you dislike?

Today's TV Commercials

How have television commercials changed over time? To begin with, television ads for cigarettes have been banned since the 1970s. And while commercials for alcohol exist, they are not allowed to show people actually drinking.

We see more commercials now than we did in the 1960s. Back then, an hour-long television program in the United States would be made up of 51 minutes of a television show, and nine minutes of commercials. Now, a typical television program runs 42 minutes, with 18 minutes devoted to commercials! As you work through the rest of this unit, ask yourself what else about television commercials has changed.

Directions: View two current television commercials at home or at school. Deconstruct each by answering the questions below.

1. Who paid for this television commercial?

   _____

2. To what age group, economic group, and gender does this commercial appeal?

   _____

   _____

3. What techniques of persuasion are used in this commercial?

   _____

   _____

4. What kind of lifestyle is presented? How is it glamorized?

   _____

   _____

5. What is the obvious message in this commercial?

   _____

6. What are the hidden messages in this commercial?

   _____

7. In what ways is this commercial a healthy or unhealthy example of media?

   _____

   _____

Below, describe what you noticed about these contemporary commercials. What is interesting about them? What do you like? What do you dislike?

_____

_____

_____

_____

Compare and Contrast

Now that you have viewed at least four television commercials, two from the past, and two from the present, think about how they have changed over time.

Directions: In the space below, complete the Venn diagram to show how past and present commercials differ. Also, explain how they are similar. Try to show how people or products have changed, and comment on music, scenery, pacing, and voices. In the television on the left, write features of the commercials from the past. In the television on the right, write features of the contemporary commercials. Where the two televisions overlap, write features that are common to both.

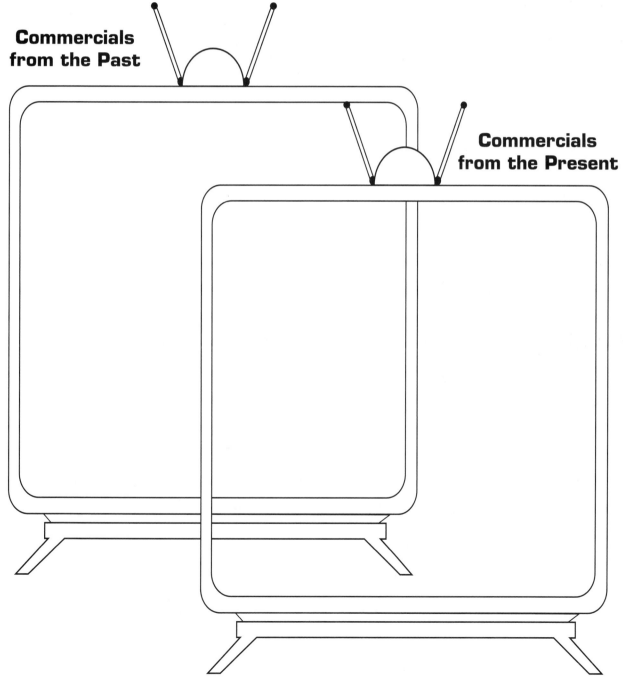

Commercials from the Past

Commercials from the Present

Create Your Commercial

Knowing the power of a television commercial, get inspired to film one of your own! You will need several sheets of lined paper, a pen or pencil, a video recorder or computer with video recording capability, and costumes and props.

Directions: In a group of three-to-four, decide what product or service you will sell on your commercial. Will you tell a story? Sing a song? Do a dance? How will you entice people to buy your product?

Write up a script for your commercial. Decide who will play which part. Decide on a director and actors. For format ideas, type the words *television script* into your favorite Internet search engine.

Consider if you will need costumes and props and obtain or make these as needed. After practicing, record your commercial. You may need to record several takes.

Deconstruct your television commercial by answering the questions below.

1. What product or idea does your commercial sell?

   _____

2. Who is your target audience?

   _____

3. What techniques of persuasion do you use in this commercial?

   _____

4. What kind of lifestyle is presented in your commercial? How is it glamorized?

   _____

5. What obvious messages exist in your commercial?

   _____

6. What hidden messages, if any, exist in your commercial?

   _____

   _____

7. How is your commercial an example of healthy or unhealthy media?

   _____

   _____

Finally, pop some popcorn and play your television commercial for your class!

Your Television Journal

How important is television in your life? Do you watch it every day, or can you not remember the last time you turned on the television?

Directions: For the next week, fill out the television journal below.

Date and Time	What I Watched	Length of Time I Watched

If you don't have a television in your household, please write a page explaining why, adding your opinions of television, and why you would prefer to have a television, or not.

News on Television

Many people all over the world wake up to the morning news on television. Others come home from work or school and turn on the news. Television news broadcasts have been around since 1948. Since that time, reporters have covered wars and sporting events, elections and grand openings, health issues, and human interest stories.

Critics say that televised news is sensational. It uses dramatic stories to get people to tune in. "If it bleeds, it leads," is a phrase used to show that news broadcasts usually begin with the most exciting story.

Directions: Watch the first five minutes of three different news programs on television. Record your findings on the chart below. The first one has been done for you.

Name of News Program	Topic of Lead Story	Description of Lead Story
KDZX News at 5	House burned down	A young couple that had just bought their first house and had their first baby came home from the hospital to find that their home had burned down.

Healthy TV News?

How does what you see on television news affect you? Which stories are healthy forms of media? Which are unhealthy?

Directions: Watch one half hour of news on television. Fill out the chart below showing all the news stories in that half hour. An example has been given for you to follow.

Name of news program watched: _____

Topic	Description	Healthy or Unhealthy?
Cat returns	Pet cat travels across the country and finds owners after a year.	Healthy. This is a feel good piece that makes people happy.

The Role of Sponsors

In the past unit, you learned about television commercials. Sponsors are people or companies who pay television stations for putting their commercial on the air.

Have you ever noticed that commercials for toys run during cartoons? Commercials for cars and trucks air during football, and ads for makeup and health products run during soap operas.

Sponsors are smart. They study who watches which programs on television. Then, they place their commercials right where their target audiences will see them!

Directions: To better understand the role of sponsors, watch a half-hour television program at home or at school. Take notes on the products you see advertised and answer the questions below.

Name of television program: _____

Products advertised in the commercials: _____

_____

1. To what age group, economic group, and gender does this television program appeal?

_____

_____

_____

2. What products were advertised most often?

_____

_____

_____

3. How do these products tie in with the program you watched and with its intended audience?

_____

_____

_____

_____

_____

_____

Messages in Television

At this point, you should understand how to find the obvious message in a piece of media. You also should know how to find the hidden message. Can you put your skills into practice, using a half-hour television program?

Directions: Review the television program you watched for the assignment on page 64, or watch another half-hour television program. In the spaces below, list all of the obvious messages and all of the hidden messages you see in the program.

Obvious Messages	Hidden Messages

Turning Off Your TV

On average, students in the United States watch 1,023 hours of television every year. While television can teach viewers amazing things, it has also been linked to poor health.

National TV-Turnoff Week began in 1994 to address the negative effects of watching television. During the last week of April every year, thousands of people across the country turn off their television sets for a week. The next three pages will help you to conduct your own TV-Turnoff Week and study the effects.

Directions: Complete the exercises below to help you understand your relationship with television.

1. On a scale of 1–10, rate the importance of television in your life. A score of 1 means that television is not important at all; a 10 means that it is very important. _____

2. Explore one group that is part of this national move to turn off your television. Using the Internet, type the following words into a search engine: *TV turnoff, turn off your television*, or *television turnoff*. Study the home page of one group's website, then answer the following questions.

1. Who paid for this website?	
2. Who might enjoy this website?	
3. Who might object to this website?	
4. What is the obvious message on their home page?	
5. What are the hidden messages on their home page?	
6. In your opinion, is this website healthy or unhealthy? Explain in detail.	

Alternatives to Television

What do you do when you're not watching television? Do you ride your bike, walk your dog, or take a dance class? What would you do if you had to give up your favorite show? Would you learn another language? Record a song you wrote? Paint a mural on your wall?

Directions: Alone, or in groups of two-to-three, brainstorm 20 activities that kids can do instead of watching television. Write them in the spaces below.

Alternatives to Television

1. _____

2. _____

3. _____

4. _____

5. _____

6. _____

7. _____

8. _____

9. _____

10. _____

11. _____

12. _____

13. _____

14. _____

15. _____

16. _____

17. _____

18. _____

19. _____

20. _____

TV-Turnoff Week Journal

For the next week, try to watch little to no television. Keep a journal in the space below. Write down how you felt every day about not watching TV, and what you did instead.

JOURNAL

Day One _____

....
....
....
....
....

Day Two _____

....
....
....
....
....

Day Three _____

....
....
....
....
....

Day Four _____

....
....
....
....
....

Day Five _____

....
....
....
....
....

Day Six _____

....
....
....
....
....

Day Seven _____

....
....
....
....
....

Music

People hear music almost as soon as they are born. Baby toys play songs like "Row, Row, Row Your Boat." Parents sing lullabies like "Rock-a-Bye Baby." Music is an important part of our life. It is also a form of media that surrounds us every day.

Directions: Complete the sentences below to analyze your relationship to music.

1. My favorite type of music is _____

    _____

2. My favorite song is _____

    _____

3. My favorite singer is _____

    _____

4. I like to listen to music when I am _____

    _____

5. I do not like to listen to music when I am _____

    _____

6. When I am in a bad mood, music _____

    _____

7. When I am in a good mood, music _____

    _____

Controversy in Music

Music as a form of media has always created controversy. Here are a few examples:

- In 1790, W.A. Mozart's opera, *Cosi Fan Tutte*, failed to impress the audience in Vienna. The audience was outraged at his portrayal of wild women.
- In the 1800s, African slaves forced to work in the fields developed a style of singing called the blues. Slave owners looked down on this type of music for good reason; often, slaves sang in codes to plan their escapes.
- In the early 1900s, people said that Ragtime music turned young people bad. The syncopated beat was blamed for listeners' drinking, dancing, and wild parties.
- In the early 21st century, people once again blamed poor behavior in young people on a form of music. This time, they condemned rap music.

One of the major controversies in the technological age has to do with file sharing. This means that a listener can buy a piece of music, put it on his or her computer, and then other people can hear this music and record it for free.

Directions: To understand the controversy about file sharing, answer the questions below.

1. How would you as a listener benefit from file sharing? How might you be harmed?

   _____

   _____

2. How would you as a musician benefit from people file sharing your music? How might you be harmed? _____

   _____

3. Now, think about a recent controversy you have heard of as it relates to music. Using your own knowledge, or newspapers and magazines, as well as the Internet, describe a recent music controversy in the space below.

Analyze a Song

Many media consumers simply listen to songs for the instruments. Often, they don't pay much attention to what the singer is saying!

Directions: Choose your favorite song. Write the lyrics in the space below. Then, answer the questions.

1. What is this song about?

2. To what age group and gender does this song appeal?

3. What kind of lifestyle does this song present? Is it glamorized? If so, how?

4. What messages did you find in this song?

5. In what ways is this song a healthy or unhealthy example of media?

Music Videos

One very popular form of media is the music video. These are two-to-three minute movies created by bands to illustrate a song. The first short music videos appeared on television in the 1980s. These days, most major bands record at least one music video for every album they put out.

Directions: You can analyze a music video as a form of media. Read the screenplay of a short video below. Then answer the questions.

Fade in:
Shows two young boys leaving their mother's tiny, broken-down cottage and wandering away from their house and into the forest to find food.

Band Appears
They all wear black. They sing grimly on a stage surrounded by dark, eerie trees. The drummer has moss hanging from her hat. There is a black spider on the arm of the lead guitarist.

Song
"So don't wander off without me, baby.
Pay attention to me, my friend.
If you wander off without me baby,
You just might reach the end."

Pan in:
Boys are lost in a dark forest. They drop to their knees, looking for footprints.

Close–up:
Lightning flashes across the sky. The boys look at each other as huge raindrops begin to fall.

1. What type of person would enjoy this music video?
   _____

2. What techniques of persuasion do you find in this video? _____
   _____

3. How would you describe the two different lifestyles presented in this video? Which is more glamorous?
   _____
   _____
   _____

4. What is the obvious message in this video? How do the little lost boys reinforce that message?
   _____
   _____
   _____

5. Do you find a hidden message in this video? If so, describe it.
   _____
   _____

72

Music Videos *(cont.)*

Do you think music videos are purely entertaining? Actually, they use symbolism, hidden messages, beautiful people, and many other techniques—just as in any form of media.

Directions: Deconstruct your favorite music video. At home or at school, watch the video, and take notes. Then, pretend you are a music critic for a magazine or newspaper. Write a review of this music video. In your report, be sure to include the following points.

- band name
- name of song in video
- audience
- lifestyle presented

- obvious message
- hidden message
- healthy or unhealthy example of media

The Times

WEDNESDAY   • FRONT PAGE •   NEWS

Make a Music Video

Now that you understand all that goes into a music video, create one of your own! You will need several sheets of lined paper, a pen or pencil, a video recorder or computer with video-recording capability, and costumes and props.

Directions: In a group of five-to-six, decide what song you will use. Will you make a video for someone else's song? Or will you come up with your own song and create a music video for it?

Write up a script for your video. Decide who will play which part. Decide on a director, actors, and band members and singers. Think about if you will need costumes and props and obtain these as needed.

Practice the video, then record it. You may need to record several takes, switching back and forth between filming your band members and singers and filming your actors.

Once complete, deconstruct your music video by recording an interview. Choose one person from your group to be the interviewer. He or she will ask several, or all, of the questions below. The other people in your group should answer them on camera! Take time to think of answers before recording.

1. What is your music video about? _____

2. Who is your target audience? _____

3. What techniques of persuasion do you use in this video? _____
    _____

4. What kind of lifestyle is presented in your video? How is it glamorized? _____
    _____

5. What obvious messages exist in your video? _____
    _____

6. What hidden messages, if any, exist in your video? _____
    _____

7. How is your music video an example of healthy or unhealthy media? _____
    _____

Finally, play your music video and interview for your class!

Videogames

Videogames have been around since the early 1970s. The first arcade videogame was called *Computer Space*. *Space Invaders*, *PacMan*, and *Centipede* began to pack arcades. In 1972, the Magnavox Odyssey let people play videogames on their own televisions. Then, kids played games with simple graphics such as *Pong*—games that required large, clunky joysticks.

These days, videogames are highly sophisticated. They allow players to enter fantastic worlds through vivid graphics and sound effects.

Videogame Console from 1970s	Contemporary Console

Directions: Study the picture of the videogame console from the 1970s. Then, look at the picture of a contemporary videogame console. Explain in a few sentences how these consoles have changed, then answer the questions.

1. _____
   _____
   _____

2. Why do you think people like to play videogames?
   _____
   _____

3. How often do you play videogames?
   _____
   _____

4. What is your favorite videogame? Why?
   _____
   _____

5. If you do not play videogames, explain why.
   _____
   _____

Videogame Ads

People who create advertisements for videogames know that their ads must be fast-paced and eye-catching. They know that videogame players like exciting graphics. Somehow, they have to convince this audience to choose their game over the hundreds of others that exist!

Directions: Study the print advertisement for a videogame below. Then, answer the questions.

1. What is the name of this videogame?

   _____

2. What company makes this videogame?

   _____

3. What is this company's slogan?

   _____

4. What is the obvious message of this print ad?

   _____

   _____

5. What is the hidden message of this print ad?

   _____

   _____

6. Is this a healthy or unhealthy form of media?

   _____

   _____

Videogame Ads *(cont.)*

Using what you have learned so far in *Media Literacy*, deconstruct one advertisement for a videogame.

Directions: Locate an ad for a videogame. This may be a print ad from a newspaper or magazine. It may be a television commercial or an Internet website. Use the questions below to deconstruct the advertisement.

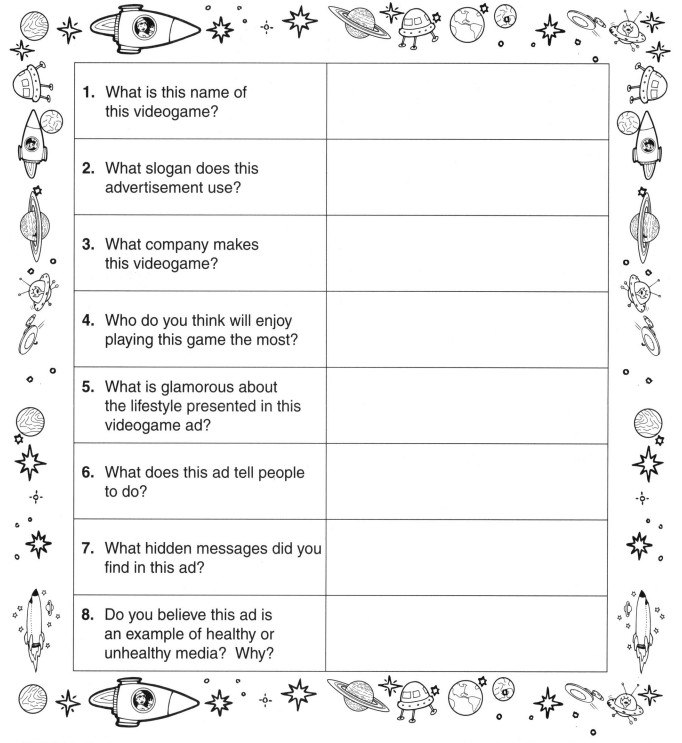

1. What is this name of this videogame?	
2. What slogan does this advertisement use?	
3. What company makes this videogame?	
4. Who do you think will enjoy playing this game the most?	
5. What is glamorous about the lifestyle presented in this videogame ad?	
6. What does this ad tell people to do?	
7. What hidden messages did you find in this ad?	
8. Do you believe this ad is an example of healthy or unhealthy media? Why?	

Violence in Videogames

Shooting aliens. Blasting bad guys. Karate-chopping the opponent. Anyone who plays videogames will be struck by the violence of many games. In one, it is the player's job to run down pedestrians. Players who complete all levels of this game have "killed" thousands of people. In 1998, researchers found that 80 percent of young people's favorite videogames had some sort of violence.

Directions: Think about your favorite videogame. Is it violent? Why do you prefer it to other games? Complete the sentences below with detailed answers.

1. My favorite videogame is _____

2. The point of this videogame is to _____

   _____

   _____

3. I like this videogame in particular because _____

   _____

   _____

4. This videogame could be considered violent because _____

   _____

   _____

5. My feelings about violence in the real world are _____

   _____

   _____

6. My feelings about violence in video games are _____

   _____

   _____

7. I think many people my age like violent video games because _____

   _____

   _____

   _____

Physical Effects

When you play video games, what do you notice about your body and your emotions? Does anything change?

Directions: For 10 minutes, play a videogame. You may choose to do this on a classroom computer, at home, or at a friend's house. Then, answer the questions below.

1. What game did you play?

   _____

   _____

2. What was the point of the videogame?

   _____

   _____

3. How did you change physically while you played? (Did your heart pound? Did your head hurt? Did you feel full of energy? Did your hands sweat?)

   _____

   _____

4. How did you change emotionally while you played? (Did you feel happy? Angry? Tense? Excited?)

   _____

   _____

   _____

Now, play 10 more minutes of a videogame, paying even closer attention to your physical and emotional reactions. Answer the questions below.

5. How is this videogame violent, if at all?

   _____

   _____

   _____

6. Did playing this game make you feel violent? Explain your answer.

   _____

   _____

   _____

7. Do you think that violence should be allowed in videogames? Explain your answer.

   _____

   _____

   _____

Your Favorite Videogame

Now that you have a good understanding of video games as a form of media, look at one game in particular.

Directions: Choose your favorite videogame to analyze. Pretend you are writing a review of it for your favorite gaming magazine. In your review, make sure to note the following details.

- brand name and name of videogame
- who will enjoy the game
- what type of world you enter into through this game
- how techniques of persuasion are used in this game
- the obvious and hidden messages in this game
- whether you believe this game to be a healthy or unhealthy form of media

Videogame Debate

Videogames cause a great deal of controversy. A classroom debate will help you to decide how you feel about this popular form of media. You will need several sheets of paper, pencils or pens, and a wristwatch or clock with a second hand.

Directions: Form two groups. One group will speak in support of videogames. The other group will speak against them.

In your group, debate the topics below. Write down any arguments you have to support your position on videogames. For instance, in the violence topic, if you are in favor of these games, you might argue that playing them keeps kids busy so that they don't get into fights. If you are against them, you might say that playing games makes kids angry and more likely to argue.

Whenever possible, back up your debate with facts, statistics, and anecdotes. This will help you to make your point clearly and persuasively.

Within your group, delegate a speaker for each topic. The remaining students can support one of the speakers. Then the speakers need to practice arguments to support the position of the group ready for the debate.

Debate Topics

- violence

- relationships with friends and family

- exercise

- effects on body and emotions

Now that your group has gathered their thoughts, it's time to debate. Your teacher will act as your moderator. Choose one person from each group to be the speaker for the first topic. Finally, select a group, through a coin toss, to go first.

When the moderator calls out a topic, the speaker from the first group has one minute to make an argument. At the end of the minute, the speaker from the second group has a minute to argue the opposing view.

Then, select another person from your group to act as the speaker for the next topic. This time, the second group goes first and has one minute to present views on the next topic, and so on. Be sure to leave five minutes at the end for both groups to discuss videogames as a whole.

Packaging

Everything comes in a package. In the morning, you reach for a cereal box or a bag of bread. These are packages. A tube of toothpaste is a package. So is a jar of store-bought jam and a can of juice.

Packages are a form of media. We see them every day. They give us clues about what is inside a container, and whether or not we want to consume it.

Here are a few details that designers must think about when they create a new package.

- shape
- color
- pictures
- text
- size

- slogan
- graphics
- name
- font

In the sixteenth century, merchants began to wrap their products in paper. They wrote the product's name on the outside of the package. By the 1700s, people sold groceries in bottles or jars with labels glued to the outside. Today, machines print out thousands of peanut butter labels at a time. But in the past, each label was handmade. In fact, even the jars were handmade!

82

Packages of the Past

You know that packages have been around for hundreds of years. What did they look like back then? Were they an effective form of media?

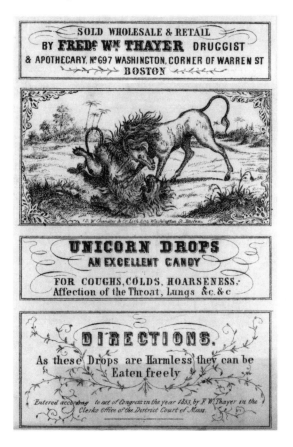

Phrase Bank
- you'll be as strong as a unicorn
- F.W. Thayer
- a battle scene with a glamorous unicorn overcoming a lion
- eat these for coughs, colds, and hoarseness
- people who are ill

Image courtesy of the Library of Congress, Prints and Photographs Division (LC-USZ62-47345)

Directions: Study the package for unicorn drops, created in 1853. Deconstruct the package by copying the correct phrase from the Phrase Bank into each blank space below.

1. This package was paid for by _____

2. This package would appeal to _____

   _____

3. The obvious message of this package is _____

   _____

4. The hidden message of this package is _____

   _____

5. The lifestyle on this package shows _____

   _____

Packages of Today

Packages surround you, every day. Can you decode what the designer wants you to think or feel when you see a box, carton, tube, bottle, or can?

Directions: Choose your favorite package to analyze. Draw it in the space below. Then, deconstruct it by answering the questions.

1. Who paid for this package?

   _____

2. What is it about this package that would appeal to a particular age group and gender?

   _____

3. What obvious message do you see in this package?

   _____

4. What hidden message do you see in this package?

   _____

5. What lifestyle is presented in this package? How is it glamorized?

   _____

6. How is this a healthy or unhealthy example of media?

   _____

Color, Shape, and Text

What color should you make a box in which to package a computer? Should a box of chocolates be square or circular? How much writing should you put on a package of poster paints? Advertising specialists and designers must ask themselves these questions about every package they create.

Directions: Study the design facts below. Then, answer the questions.

Design Facts

- The color blue is calming to buyers.
- The colors red, yellow, and orange arouse hunger in buyers.
- The color green symbolizes friendliness to the Earth.
- The color purple stands out as mysterious.
- A product stands out as desirable if the package includes plenty of information.
- An unusually-shaped package is interesting to buyers.
- Children generally like cartoon and superhero characters on packages.

Questions

1. What color would you make a package that holds a microscope with some assembly required?

   _____

2. What package shape might you create for a kids' board game to make it stand out to buyers?

   _____

3. What color would you make a bottle that holds non-toxic craft glue? _____

4. What color would you make a bag that holds a wizard's costume? _____

5. What image would you put on a box of kids' cereal? _____

6. What color might you make a packet that holds chocolate-covered peanuts? _____

7. What kind of information would you put on a box that holds an action figure from a new movie?

   _____

   _____

   _____

   _____

Compare and Contrast

Earlier in this unit, you looked at packages from the past and present. Now, study them with a critical eye to see how they have changed over the centuries.

Directions: Examine each package shown on page 87. Deconstruct these by answering the questions, and then complete the essay assignment.

Label One

1. What is this product? What is the brand name?

   _____

2. What stands out about the text on this package label?

   _____

3. What stands out about the image on this package label?

   _____

4. What does this package label promise buyers?

   _____

5. What slogan does this package use?

   _____

Label Two

6. What is this product? What is the brand name?

   _____

7. What stands out about the text on this package label?

   _____

8. What stands out about the image on this package label?

   _____

9. What does this package label promise buyers?

   _____

10. What slogan does this package use?

    _____

11. In this unit, you have observed how packaging has changed over the centuries. You have also seen that some aspects of packaging remain the same. On a separate sheet of paper, write a short essay to compare and contrast packages from the past and present. Pay attention to text, images, slogans, promises, and brand names as you write your essay.

Label One

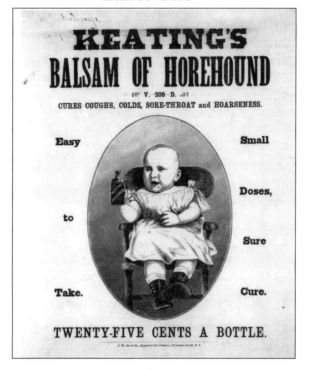

Image courtesy of the Library of Congress, Prints and Photographs Division (LC-USZ62-51231)

Label Two

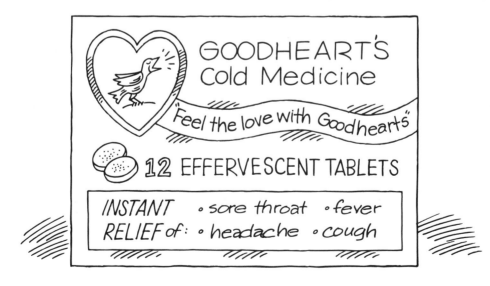

Design Your Own Package

From this unit, you have learned how package designers pay close attention to text, images, slogans, brands, colors, and other parts of a box, can, bottle, tube, or carton. Now, you can design a package of your own. This project can be completed individually or in groups.

Materials

- scratch paper
- pencil with eraser
- construction paper
- scissors

- glue or tape
- markers or colored pencils
- ruler (optional)

Directions

1. Decide the product you will package. Begin by sketching your idea for a package on scratch paper. Make sure to come up with a brand name, a slogan, text, images, and anything else you think will help to sell your product.

2. Decide on a size, color (or colors), and shape for your package.

3. Once you have a solid design for your package, create it out of construction paper. Fold your package into a three-dimensional shape (see below) and glue or tape it.

4. Draw text and images, brand name and slogan on your package with markers or colored pencils..

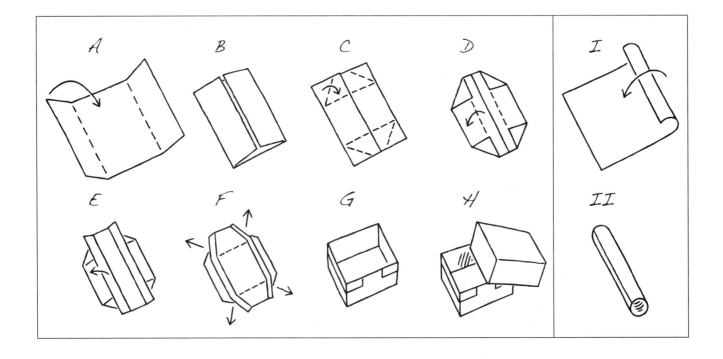

Product Placement Happens

Have you ever watched a movie and noticed that the star wears a particular brand of shoes and drinks a specific kind of soda? Have you played a videogame and found that the main character wears a certain label on his jacket and hat? Have you opened a kids' book to find that the characters are eating a particular type of cookie?

Product placement is the deliberate placing of a specific brand-name item in some form of media. Below are a few examples.

- a character in your favorite television show is always drinking Diet Coke®

- the song, "Take Me Out to the Ball Game" mentions buying Cracker Jacks®

- a picture book that teaches kids to count uses pictures of M & Ms®

- your favorite videogame asks you to take characters to Pizza Hut®

- the main characters in your favorite movie wear Ray-Ban® sunglasses

So how is product placement different from an advertisement? An ad gives consumers an obvious message—you need this product. A product placed in a movie, book, song, TV show, or videogame offers a more hidden message. Advertisers hope that consumers will buy something simply because they've seen it used in one of these forms of media.

Product Placement Methods

Advertisers hope that placement of their product will appear so naturally in media that people will be attracted to brand names without even being aware that they have seen them.

There are three ways that product placement occurs.

1. Sometimes, it just happens thanks to suggestions from an actor, director, or set decorator. Product placement can give movies, television, and other forms of media a realistic touch. Can you relate more to a character who is eating from a bag marked "Potato Chips," or more to one who snacks from a bag marked with a specific brand-name?

2. Other times, product placement is the result of a trade. A television director promises to feature one brand of bottled water in a program if the company promises unlimited bottled water to the program's cast and crew.

3. Finally, there are some times when product placement is purchased. The makers of a sports shoe pay a movie producer a certain amount of money to make sure that the main character in the film wears their sports shoes with the brand name displayed for audiences to read.

Directions: On television or on the Internet, watch a movie preview, no longer than three minutes. You can find hundreds of previews by typing the words *movie trailer* into your favorite search engine. Then, in the space below, write down every brand-name product you observed in the preview.

Name of movie being previewed _____

Product placed within the preview

Products in Books

One of the largest forms of media to feature product placement is children's learning books. Little kids might learn to count by studying pictures of brand-name candies and cookies on the pages of books designed just for them.

Directions: Study the pages from a children's counting book below. Then, deconstruct them by answering the questions.

1. How are candy bars used in this book?

   _____

   _____

2. How do you think this product placement occurred?

   _____

   _____

3. What age group will enjoy this book?

   _____

   _____

4. What obvious thing will readers learn from this book?

   _____

   _____

5. What hidden thing might readers learn from this book?

   _____

   _____

6. How is this counting book an example of healthy or unhealthy media?

   _____

   _____

Products in Videogames

Product placement in videogames has been around since the 1980s. One game from 1989 featured a national pizza chain. Another game showed the cartoon mascot from a popular soft drink. The bananas in a 2001 videogame have stickers with a particular company's name on them. And the games of today show the names of fast food restaurants, brand-name cellular phones, and even a specific brand of surfboard wax!

Directions: Answer the questions below for a better understanding of product placement in videogames.

1. Why do you think advertisers want to put their products in videogames?

   _____

   _____

2. Why do you think videogame designers agree to feature name-brand products in their games?

   _____

   _____

3. Do you think players like or dislike product placement in videogames? Explain your answer.

   _____

   _____

4. How do you think players are affected by the placement of specific products such as pizza and soft drinks in their games?

   _____

   _____

Now, think like a videogame designer. In the space below, draw a scene from a videogame you have made up. Include at least three examples of product placement, making sure to write the name of each brand on your product.

Products on Television

Many children's television programs include placement of products that appeal to kids. Advertisers hope viewers will recognize and buy these products.

Directions: Choose a children's program, between 30 and 60 minutes in length, from a television network aimed at young people. Watch the program carefully, and see how many name-brand products you can find. Write them down in the space below and explain how they are used. For example, you might write: "Jordan picks up a can of Rocky's Root Beer. There is a close-up on his Watusi-brand wristwatch."

Pay particular attention to brand-name clothing, shoes, hats, food and drink, computers and videogames, cellular phones, stores, restaurants, athletic equipment, and toys.

Taste-Test

Is name-brand soda really tastier than the generic version or do consumers simply believe what advertisers tell them?

Hold a blind taste-test to determine what soda you find tastier. If you prefer, you may use name-brand and generic fruit juice, or bottled and tap water.

Materials:

- one liter bottle of name brand non-caffeinated soda
- one liter bottle of a generic version of the same soda
- two brown paper grocery sacks
- scissors

- masking tape
- a pen
- small paper cups, two for each student
- scrap paper, one small piece for each student
- receptacle for scrap paper—bowl or hat or paper bag

Directions: Assign one person—preferably the teacher—to be the tester. Cut the grocery sacks to fit around each liter bottle. Affix them with tape so that people cannot read the labels on the bottles. On one bottle, write *Soda One*. On the other, write *Soda Two*.

Now it's time to line up for a taste test. Everyone but the first student should remain five feet away from the tester. The tester pours a little soda from the first bottle into a cup. The first student drinks it. The tester pours a little soda from the second bottle for the student to taste.

When the student has tasted both kinds of soda, he or she writes down the preferred bottle—number one or number two on a piece of scrap paper and folds it, then puts it in the bowl or bag.

There must be no discussion among students in order to get accurate results from this taste test. When the first student is finished, invite the next student to taste both sodas, and so on.

When everyone has finished tasting, tally up students' preferences. Then, take the labels off of the soda bottles and discuss the following questions with your class.

1. Were you surprised by which soda the class preferred?

2. What were the differences between the two sodas tasted?

3. Why might someone choose to buy a name-brand soda over the generic soda?

4. Why might someone choose to buy a generic soda over the name-brand soda?

5. How do you think product placement affects students?

Products in Movies

As you studied and recorded product placement in television programs, you can also study and chart the placement of name-brand items in your favorite movies.

Directions: Choose a feature-length film. Watch it carefully and take notes on how many name-brand products you can find. Write down the products in the space below and explain how they are used. For example, you might write: "In the movie "Seventh-Grade Soccer Camp," Sarah wears Player-brand cleats and a shirt with the Player logo. She uses a Great Goalie soccer ball and drinks Thirstygirl sports drinks."

Pay particular attention to brand-name clothing, shoes, hats, food and drink, computers and videogames, cellular phones, stores, restaurants, athletic equipment, and toys.

Magazines

There are thousands of magazines all over the world, and each of them represents media. Magazines for young people first appeared in the United States during the mid-1900s. Now, such magazines exist all over the world, in numerous languages.

Different magazines cover different topics. Some publish stories and photos that relate to music, television, and movies. Some focus on pets such as cats, dogs, birds, or horses. Some provide information on sports or cars, and others are lifestyle magazines for young people that include all of the above.

Girls most often buy these lifestyle magazines. Boys frequently buy magazines related to specific activities such as bicycling or backpacking. However, both boys and girls are profoundly influenced by the images they see in magazines.

Directions: Study this magazine cover from 1898 and answer the questions below. You may need to use books or the Internet to find some of the answers.

Image courtesy of The National Archives (533225)

1. What is the name of this magazine? _____

2. To what gender and age group did this magazine cover appeal? _____

3. What war was taking place during 1898? _____

4. What is the obvious message of this magazine cover?

   _____

5. What is the hidden message of this magazine cover?

   _____

6. What does the flag on this cover symbolize?

   _____

7. What does the bugle on this cover symbolize?

   _____

Tricks in Photography

Why does that chocolate cake look perfect on the front cover of a magazine, but when you make it at home, it is smaller and lopsided? Why do those two kids in the photo about snowboarding look gorgeous, but you come in off the slopes with messed-up hair and chapped skin?

Magazine photographers use all sorts of methods to make sure their subject looks fantastic. Here are some of their favorite tricks.

- To make a Fourth of July picnic look picture-perfect in a food magazine, a food stylist may spray the food with a mixture of water and corn syrup so that those hamburgers and hot dogs glisten.

- To show a steaming bowl of soup on the front cover of a woman's magazine, photographers might soak cotton balls in water, and then microwave them and place them out of sight behind the bowl of soup to create steam.

- The cover model with the smooth, radiant skin and dark hair may actually have pockmarked skin and purple hair. However, magazine photographers can airbrush pictures so that skin looks good, and they can even change someone's hair color from purple to black using a computer program!

- The incredibly thin actor in the magazine story on eating disorders may not actually be so skinny. Photographers may have put the actor's head on another person's body to add drama to the story.

- The nature magazine that shows a peregrine falcon catching a sparrow in its talons may have relied on digital enhancement. This lets a photographer combine a photo of a sparrow with a photo of a peregrine falcon to make it look like a dramatic capture.

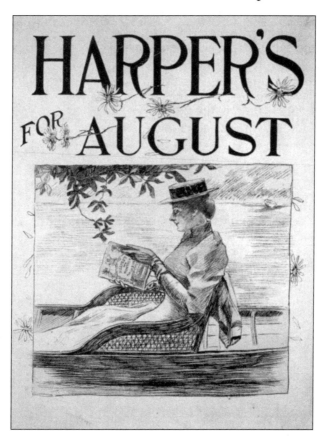

Image courtesy of the Library of Congress, Prints and Photographs Division (LC-USZC2-517)

Tricks in Photography (cont.)

Now that you understand how photographers can enhance or change images, examine the effects of these tricks on consumers.

Directions: Read each scenario. Circle the letter or letters that best explain the possible effects of the scenario.

1. A young woman hoping to model for fashion magazines studies the photos in several of her favorites. She sees that the models are very tall, thin, and beautiful. She herself is of average weight and height, and she has a large nose. The young woman
   a. goes to the doctor and gets nose-reduction surgery.
   b. decides not to be a model after all and starts looking for a different career she will enjoy.
   c. feels bad about herself and resolves to eat only one meal a day.
   d. none of the above.

2. A boy who wants to go to culinary school wants to make a cheese soufflé of the sort he sees on the cover of his favorite magazine. However, he cannot get his cheese soufflés to look like the perfect, golden-brown steaming image in the magazine. The boy
   a. gives up on cooking and decides to be a doctor instead.
   b. feels like a failure and throws his soufflés in the trash.
   c. tries over and over again to make a picture-perfect soufflé, even more determined to be a chef.
   d. none of the above.

3. A young man who has the same height and weight as his favorite actor also wants his amazing leg muscles. No matter how much he runs and lifts weights, however, his legs remain very thin. The young man
   a. feels inadequate and stops going to the gym.
   b. decides to work out at the gym with a personal trainer to get the look he wants.
   c. stops exercising and watches TV all afternoon.
   d. none of the above.

4. A girl who loves to knit attempts to make a hat she saw in her favorite craft magazine. She tries three times, but her own hats come out lumpy and lopsided instead of perfect like the photo. The girl
   a. stops knitting because she can't do it perfectly.
   b. cries and throws her hats in the garbage.
   c. wears her best creation, knowing she tried her best to make it and is proud of that.
   d. none of the above.

Magazines for Children

Over the next two pages, you'll compare and contrast two magazines designed specifically for young people in order to become literate consumers of this type of media.

Directions: Choose one magazine from the first list and one magazine from the second list. You may choose to compare these in print form, or on the Internet. Use the chart below to show the comparisons.

List One	List Two
Teen Voices	Seventeen
Skipping Stones	YM
The Writer's Slate	National Geographic Kids
Cat Fancy	CosmoGirl!
Dog Fancy	Girls' Life
New Moon Publishing	Elle Girl
Cobblestone	Teen Vogue
Boys' Life	American Girl

Question	Magazine One	Magazine Two
What is the name of this magazine?		
To what gender, age group, and economic group does this magazine appeal?		
What kind of lifestyle is presented? How is it glamorized?		
What are the obvious messages in this magazine?		
What are the hidden messages in this magazine?		
What techniques of persuasion are used in this magazine?		
How is this magazine a healthy or unhealthy example of media?		

Finally, write a paragraph comparing and contrasting these two magazines.

99

Messages in Magazines

Magazines for children and young adults have long been criticized for the messages they send to readers.

Directions: Study the magazine covers below and on page 101. Then, answer the questions.

1. What stands out about this magazine cover?

   _____
   _____
   _____

2. What obvious messages will a reader see right away when looking at this cover?

   _____
   _____
   _____

3. What hidden messages might readers find if they think deeper about this cover?

   _____
   _____
   _____

4. In a single paragraph, explain how this magazine cover is a healthy or unhealthy example of media.

   _____
   _____
   _____

1. What stands out about this magazine cover?

   _____

   _____

2. What obvious messages will a reader see right away when looking at this cover?

   _____

   _____

3. What hidden messages might readers find if they think deeper about this cover?

   _____

   _____

4. In a single paragraph, explain how this magazine cover is a healthy or unhealthy example of media.

   _____

   _____

   _____

   _____

   _____

   _____

   _____

   _____

   _____

Your Favorite Magazine

As a young person, you probably have a favorite magazine that you read often. But what really attracts you to this form of media?

Directions: Choose your favorite magazine. Then, write a letter to your best friend explaining why he or she should read this magazine, too. In your letter, make sure to include the following:

- name of magazine
- who will enjoy it
- the lifestyle presented
- techniques of persuasion
- obvious and hidden messages
- whether it is a healthy or unhealthy example of media

Date: _____

Dear _____,

_____

_____

_____

_____

_____

_____

_____

_____

_____

Sincerely,

_____

Design a Magazine

What types of images and articles go into a healthy magazine? Make one of your own, and find out! You will need scrap paper and pencils, several sheets of white or colored paper (9" x 11"), markers, stickers, glitter, glue, scissors, three-hole punch, and three metal brads, or ribbon 2' long.

Directions:

1. Decide whether you want to make a magazine as a class or in groups of three-to-four. In your group, talk about what type of magazine you want to create. Will it have a specific focus on something like skateboarding or drawing or animals, or will it be more of a general lifestyle magazine?

2. Talk about what images and articles will make this a healthy form of media. Brainstorm your ideas for your magazine in the box at the bottom of the page.

3. Assign people in the group to write articles and/or create illustrations. Decide on a layout for your magazine. Where will the articles go on each page? Where will the illustrations go?

4. Create each page of your magazine. You may want to write and draw directly on each page. Alternatively, you can write articles and draw pictures on separate pieces of paper and glue them to the main magazine page.

5. Use the three-hole punch to carefully punch holes into your magazine pages. Affix them with metal brads, or weave a ribbon through the holes and tie it in a bow.

6. In a single paragraph, deconstruct your magazine on a separate sheet of paper. Explain the intended audience, hidden and obvious messages, persuasive audience techniques, and how this magazine is a healthy example of media.

Newspapers

"Extra! Extra! Read All About It!" Newspapers provide day-to-day coverage of events for the public to read and discuss. This powerful form of media has been around since the 1400s. In Renaissance Europe, people read hand-written newspapers to learn about wars, economic conditions, and human-interest stories.

Sometimes these early newspapers were sensational. For instance, German papers reported crimes committed in Transylvania by Vlad Tsepes Drakul. Later stories called the villain Count Dracula!

In 1666, the *London Gazette* became the first English newspaper. A newspaper called *Publick Occurrences* appeared in Boston soon after. However, its publisher was arrested for distributing it without government approval and all copies of the newspaper were destroyed.

By the start of the Revolutionary War a hundred years later, people in the American colonies could read two dozen different newspapers. In fact, articles in these papers helped to push colonists toward political independence from England!

Today, we can read thousands of newspapers in print and on the Internet every day, in hundreds of languages. There are even specialty newspapers. They focus on stories relevant to a particular religion, or to the environment, or to people interested in news that is just plain weird!

Image courtesy of the Library of Congress, Prints and Photographs Division (LC-USZ62-19955)

Front Pages of the Past

In some ways, newspapers of today are very different from those published hundreds of years ago. In other ways, they are much the same.

Directions: Study the front page of the newspaper on page 106, then fill in the crossword puzzle below.

ACROSS

3. What technique of persuasion is used in the headlines?
6. Who is on this front page?
7. This front page tells readers that their country is at _____.

DOWN

1. The name of this newspaper is The _____ .
2. What technique of persuasion is used in the cartoon?
3. Which word stands out in the main headline?
4. What age group would be most interested in reading this newspaper?
5. What is found at the top of the right-hand side of the page?

Image courtesy of the Library of Congress, Prints and Photographs Division (LC-USF34-056681-D)

Front Pages of Today

Directions: Choose the front page of a contemporary newspaper. You may select one from the library, from home, school, or from the Internet. Answer the six journalism questions: Who, What, Why, Where, When, and How to deconstruct this newspaper.

Who?	Who publishes this paper? Who reads it?	
What?	What is the name of the paper? What messages do you get from it?	
Why?	Why would people want to read this paper?	
Where?	Where does this paper get printed? Where can you buy it?	
When?	When can people read this paper? Every day? Once a week?	
How?	How does this paper use techniques of persuasion to help sell copies?	

Your Local Paper

Your local newspaper can tell you so much about the city or town in which you live!

Directions: Study a copy of your local newspaper. Then, answer the questions on a separate piece of paper.

1. What is the name of this newspaper?
2. Who owns this newspaper?
3. How long has this newspaper been published?
4. What is its circulation (that is, how many readers does it have)?
5. What stories appear on the front page?
6. Which story is the most important? How can you tell?
7. Now, examine each section of your local newspaper. In the chart below, name each section, describe it, and note what types of articles it features. See the example for details.

Section	Description	Featured Articles
Food	It has recipes, advice, calendar events, restaurant reviews, and photos.	Salsa recipe, advice for cake-baking, cake recipes and photos, information about food fair, and a review of a newly opened café.

The Op/Ed Section

The Opinion/Editorial section provides a wealth of information about what's on your fellow citizens' mind. The editor of the newspaper writes the editorial(s). People from your community write opinion columns and letters to the editor.

Directions: Study one Op/Ed section of your local paper. Answer the questions below.

1. What are the topics of the editorials in this Op/Ed section?

   _____

   _____

2. What are the topics of the opinion pieces (not editorials) in this Op/Ed section?

   _____

   _____

3. What topics are mentioned in the letters to the editor in this Op/Ed section?

   _____

   _____

In a paragraph below, describe what the Op/Ed section of your local paper says about your town or city's residents and their concerns.

_____

_____

_____

_____

_____

_____

_____

_____

_____

_____

_____

_____

A Letter to the Editor

Think writing a letter to the editor and getting it published in your local newspaper is only for adults? Think again! The next two pages will show you how to write a letter and submit it to your newspaper for publication.

Directions: First, think of a community issue that concerns you as a young person. Maybe you want to write about bicycle safety. Perhaps you want to write about people who don't pick up after their dogs. Or maybe you want to write about the good deeds done by people your age.
Choose a topic and write a draft of your letter, below.

Date: _____

Dear _____,

_____

_____

_____

_____

_____

_____

_____

Sincerely,

My Name: _____

Address: _____

Phone: _____

Email: _____

A Letter to the Editor (cont.)

It's easy to submit a letter to your local newspaper editor. Sometimes, editors prefer letters submitted by e-mail. Other times, they prefer them sent through the post office. While editors don't always have the space to publish all letters, they always read them!

Directions: Study the *Letters to the Editor* page of your local newspaper. Below, write the steps you must take to submit your letter to the editor.

Now, type up the letter you wrote on page 110. Proofread it for correct spelling, punctuation, and grammar. Then, send it to the editor, following the instructions you detailed above.

Note that sometimes an editor will hold on to your letter for as long as two weeks before he or she publishes it. Other times, editors will publish a letter the day after it is received. You may have even more luck getting your letter published if you note your age beside your signature.

Spinning a Story

A *spin*, in newspaper writing, is a specific angle from which a reporter writes about a topic. For instance, a feature reporter might spin the topic of cat care to focus on why indoor cats live longer than outdoor cats. He or she might spin the topic to focus on the benefits of making your own cat food. Or a reporter might spin this topic to talk about the importance of regular brushing to prevent hairballs.

Sometimes, different countries will spin a news story in various ways. Reasons for this vary. One country may find a story very relevant while another might give it just a little coverage since it isn't important. Reporters are not supposed to put their opinions into a story. However, sometimes they put a positive or negative spin on an article. For instance, a reporter from the United States might put a positive spin on the opening of a new restaurant chain, while a reporter from France might write about it with a negative spin.

Directions: Choose one national news story from this week. Examine how this story is covered in one United States newspaper and in two other newspapers from different countries. Answer the questions below and on the next page about this news story. You can use the Internet to find international newspapers.

1. Briefly describe the topic of the national news story you have chosen.

   _____

   _____

2. Write down the names of the three newspapers in which you read about this same news story.

   _____

   _____

3. Study each article for its spin, or angle. Can you tell whether each story has a positive or negative spin? Explain your answer, below. An example has been given.

Name of Newspaper	Spin or Angle
U.S. Newspaper—The Eugene Times	Spins an article on Japanese anime to say that it is ruining traditional American cartoons. This is a negative spin on the story.

Spinning a Story (cont.)

Directions: Below, write two paragraphs comparing the same story as it appears in three different newspapers. In the first paragraph, explain how each story is the same. In the second paragraph, explain how each story is different. Pay close attention to how each reporter puts a spin on the story.

Similarities

_____

_____

_____

_____

_____

_____

Differences

_____

_____

_____

_____

_____

_____

Art

Leonardo da Vinci's "Mona Lisa." Andy Warhol's "Campbell's Soup Can." Maya Lin's Vietnam Veteran's Memorial. What do these three objects have in common? Each is a work of art. Each is also a form of media.

Prehistoric art in the form of petroglyphs can be viewed as media. Like petroglyphs, you can deconstruct paintings, sculptures, and photographs, as well.

As an example, consider photographer Dorothea Lange's 1937 photograph of an eighteen-year old migrant mother during the Great Depression. The Farm Security Administration paid for Lange to take photographs of people affected by the Depression.

Image courtesy of the Library of Congress,
Prints and Photographs Division (LC-USF34-016285-E)

Directions: Study the image above and answer these questions.

1. Who was affected by the Great Depression, and how?	
2. Who paid for this media?	
3. To what gender, age group, and economic group does this piece of art appeal?	
4. What lifestyle is presented? How is it glamorized?	
5. What obvious messages exist in this piece of art?	
6. What hidden messages exist in this piece of art?	

Painting

The history of painting goes back thousands of years. From the time the first prehistoric people painted bison and horses on cave walls until now, paintings have represented a colorful form of media. Sometimes painters use their work to show political messages, as in the painting called "Peace," shown on page 116. This is an allegorical painting—that is, a work of art that uses symbolism—about the Treaty of Ghent. America and Great Britain signed this treaty on December 24, 1814.

Directions: Study this painting by John Rubens Smith, completed in 1814. Then, answer the questions below.

1. What is happening in this painting? You may have to research the Treaty of Ghent to answer this question.

   _____

   _____

2. What symbols do you notice? Explain them in terms of what they represent.

   _____

   _____

3. What is the obvious message of this painting?

   _____

   _____

4. What is the hidden message, if any, of this painting?

   _____

   _____

5. What is the lifestyle presented in this painting? How is it glamorized?

   _____

   _____

6. Is this a healthy or unhealthy example of media?

   _____

   _____

Think about how painting has changed since Rubens Smith's time and how it has stayed the same.

Directions: Using books, encyclopedias, or the Internet, select one contemporary painting. Sketch it on a separate piece of paper.

Below your sketch, write a description of the painting. In it, explain the artist's name, what is happening in the painting, obvious and hidden messages, the particular lifestyle portrayed by this painting, and whether you believe this art to be a healthy or unhealthy form of media.

Image courtesy of the Library of Congress, Prints and Photographs Division (LC-USZC4-2675)

Sculpture

Like painting, the history of sculpture goes back to prehistoric times. Most Stone Age sculpture was made of ivory or clay. Later, Egyptians used precious metals such as gold and silver for their sculptures.

One of the most famous sculptures is the sculpture of Abraham Lincoln within the Lincoln Memorial. This sculpture was created in 1914 to honor the 16th President of the United States.

Directions: Using books, encyclopedias, and the Internet, research this sculpture, then deconstruct it by filling out the chart below.

1. Who created this sculpture, and where is it located?	
2. What types of people would enjoy looking at this sculpture?	
3. What was Lincoln's role in the Civil War, and how did he die?	
4. What obvious message do you find in the way that Abraham Lincoln is portrayed in this sculpture?	
5. Do you find any hidden meanings in this sculpture? If so, explain.	
6. What group might find this sculpture offensive?	

Sculpture *(cont.)*

Over hundreds of years, sculpture has interested people as a form of media. In 1885, Pierre August Rodin created "The Left Hand."

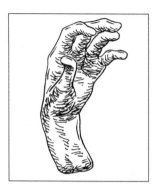

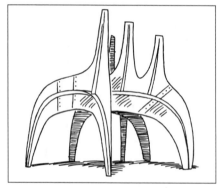

Alexander Calder created enormous shapes out of metal, such as "Red Horse."

Both of these sculptures have one thing in common—they represent media!

Directions: Create your own sculpture as a form of media. You will need a block of clay (any size or color), a small dish of water, and a craft stick for sculpting and defining.

Using your block of clay, create a sculpture. Water will help to mold your clay into a desired shape. Use the craft stick to create sharp details, if needed.

When finished, deconstruct your sculpture by answering the questions below.

1. Who is your intended audience for this sculpture?

   _____

2. What are the obvious messages of your sculpture?

   _____

   _____

3. What are the hidden messages in your sculpture?

   _____

   _____

4. How is this sculpture an example of healthy or unhealthy media?

   _____

   _____

Photography

Is a picture worth a thousand words? Since its beginning in the late 1800s, photography has been used as a form of media. It appears on the walls of art galleries. It also appears in newspapers and magazines. Consider this photograph taken in 1942.

Directions: Study the photograph below. Deconstruct it by filling out the chart below.

Image courtesy of The National Archives (537744)

1. Using the Internet, books, or encyclopedias, explain, in two or three sentences, what Japanese internment was.	
2. What do you think is happening in this photo?	
3. What obvious messages exist in this photograph?	
4. What hidden messages exist in this photograph?	
5. How does this photograph make you feel?	
6. How is this photograph a healthy or unhealthy example of media?	

How is contemporary photography used as media? What messages does it send to viewers?

Directions: Choose a photograph of one of your favorite celebrities. On a separate sheet of paper, paste or sketch it.

Now, deconstruct this photograph in one detailed paragraph. In your writing, make sure to discuss what lifestyle is presented, the hidden and obvious messages of this photograph, what type of viewer will enjoy this photograph, and whether this photo is a healthy or unhealthy example of media. Feel free to add other details that you observe.

Comic Books

The comic book format was invented in the 1930s. One of the first superheroes to appear in comics was Superman. Batman and Robin, Wonderwoman, and the Green Hornet, along with other superheroes that showed superhuman strength in the pages of comic books, followed superman.

Later, the Archie comic books appeared. They were about teenagers, and young people loved to read them. Some organizations put out comic books. They tried to convey knowledge in a colorful and interesting way. One such comic was titled "The Study of Nuclear Energy." General Electric put out this book in 1948.

Image courtesy of The National Archives (281568)

Directions: Study the front page of the comic book shown above, then fill in this chart.

1. What do you think this comic book is about?	
2. How does this comic book try to appeal to young readers?	
3. What happened in the Japanese city of Hiroshima on August 6, 1945?	
4. This comic book came out in 1948. Why do you think General Electric put out this comic book?	
5. In what ways is this comic book a healthy/unhealthy example of media?	

Comic Books *(cont.)*

The first Japanese comic books, called *manga*, appeared in the eighteenth century. Manga means "whimsical pictures."

Today, manga are sophisticated comic books, often with black and white drawings and just a few color pages. Sometimes, they inspire anime—animation that becomes part of a television program or movie.

Directions: Gather two comic books—one from the United States and one from Japan. Study each of them. Then, compare and contrast these books below.

1. What is the plot of each of these comic books? Describe them in a few sentences below:

   a. _____

   _____

   b. _____

   _____

2. Describe the art in each comic book. For instance, is it in color or black and white? How are people and animals portrayed? Are the drawings simple or complex?

   a. _____

   _____

   b. _____

   _____

3. What do you see as similar about these two comic books?

   a. _____

   _____

   b. _____

   _____

4. How are these two comic books the same?

   _____

   _____

5. Are these comic books examples of healthy or unhealthy media? Explain your answer.

   _____

   _____

Graffiti Versus Murals

What do you think when you see a bad word spray-painted on the side of a building? Do you think something different when you see a complex and colorful mural outside someone's store?

Graffiti and murals are both examples of media. The definition of graffiti is: "Initials, slogans, or drawings on a wall or sidewalk." The definition of a mural is: "A large picture on a wall or ceiling."

Directions: Study these two images, then deconstruct each form of media by completing the sentences below on a separate piece of paper. Answer the questions twice—once for each image.

1. This is a picture of _____ .

2. The technique of persuasion used in this image is _____ .

3. The obvious message of this media is _____ .

4. The artist may have created this picture in order to _____ .

Finally, in groups of three-to-four students, discuss why you think that murals are often seen in a positive light, while graffiti is seen as negative.

Create a Mural

You can create a mural to brighten your classroom!

Materials:

- scratch paper
- butcher paper, enough to cover one classroom bulletin board
- pencils with erasers
- paintbrushes, both thick and thin, one for each person
- cans of water-soluble paint in various colors
- newspaper
- clean-up rags and water
- tape or staples

Directions:

1. Cover a bulletin board with butcher paper. Tape or staple the paper to the back of the board.
2. Decide as a group what your mural will look like. You might want to design it as a class. Alternatively, break into groups of four and design a small section of the mural on your own. Sketch your designs with a pencil on scratch paper.
3. Get ready to paint! Gather rags and water for cleaning up. Spread newspaper below the wall so you don't get paint on the floor. Outline your mural design with small brushes and paint. Then, fill in the outlines with paint.
4. Allow the paint to dry and wash brushes well.
5. Deconstruct your mural by answering the questions below.

1. What gender, age group, and economic group does your mural appeal to?	
2. What kind of lifestyle is presented? How is it glamorized?	
3. What obvious messages exist in your mural?	
4. What hidden messages exist in your mural?	
5. In what ways is your mural a healthy or unhealthy example of media?	

Websites

The moment you turn on your computer and connect to the Internet, you see websites. Text, images, and advertising—all at the click of a mouse—make this form of media complex.

It is important to be literate about websites as a form of media. You need to know who is trying to sell you a product or idea. You should be aware of the effects of advertising. Being able to answer these questions will make you a media literate consumer of websites.

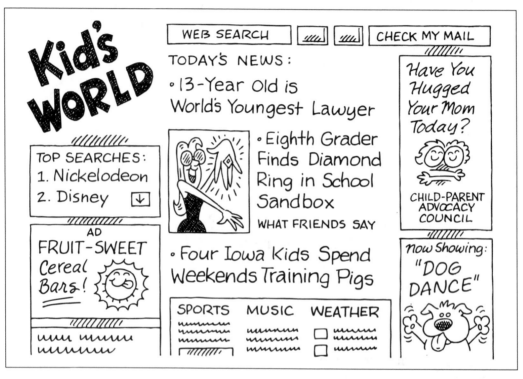

Directions: Study the sample website above. Answer the questions.

1. What gender, age group, and economic group would enjoy this webpage?

   _____

   _____

2. How many news stories do you count on this webpage?

   _____

3. How many advertisements do you count on this webpage?

   _____

4. Why was this particular photo chosen to illustrate this webpage?

   _____

   _____

5. In what ways is this webpage a healthy or unhealthy example of media?

   _____

   _____

Popular Home Pages

A home page is the opening, or main page, of a website. It serves as a "hello" to visitors and provides links to click for further information. There are hundreds of popular home pages. You may already have a favorite!

Directions: Choose one home page to deconstruct and draw it in the space below. Fill in the blanks to create a short report about it.

I am here today to talk about the home page called _____. It's a very

_____ homepage that will appeal to those who are _____

years old and make _____ money. I would describe the lifestyle on this home page

as _____.

The designer of this page used a few persuasive advertising techniques. These include

_____, _____, and _____. You can tell at

a glance that the obvious messages on this home page tell viewers to _____ and to

_____. But look carefully, and you'll also see hidden messages that tell

consumers to _____ and _____.

I urge you to study this home page for yourself. I think you will find it a _____

form of media.

Websites for Young People

Many, many websites for kids exist on the Internet. Are you interested in history? There are websites for kids who are interested in almost any type of history, from ancient Greece to politics. Passionate about horses? There are websites specifically for kids who ride and work with these animals.

Directions: Search for a kids' websites based on the list below. In your search engine, type *kids* and the name of the topic that interests you. Then, answer the questions to deconstruct this website.

- history
- nature
- math
- music
- animals
- science
- sports
- movies
- politics
- art
- books
- theater

1. What is the name of this home page?	
2. To what gender, age group, and economic group does this home page appeal?	
3. What methods of persuasion do you see on this home page?	
4. What lifestyle is presented on this home page? How is it glamorized?	
5. What are the obvious messages on this home page?	
6. What are the hidden messages on this home page?	
7. How is this home page an example of healthy or unhealthy media?	

Author Websites

By now, you have a favorite author of books for children or young adults. Many authors maintain a website on which they present photos, interviews, information on their books, and calendars to let readers know when they will be appearing in public and where.

Directions: Choose your favorite author. Locate his or her website with the help of your favorite search engine. The key words should include the author's name and the words *home page*. Below, write a letter to your author in which you discuss his or her website. What parts of the website do you like? Which do you feel could be improved?

Make observations on obvious and hidden messages on the website, as well as on whether you feel it is a healthy or unhealthy example of media.

Date: _____

Dear _____,

_____

_____

_____

_____

_____

_____

_____

_____

Sincerely,

_____

Podcasts

A podcast is an Internet-based broadcast of news and/or entertainment. You can download it on your computer and listen to it at your leisure.

There are numerous podcasts designed for young listeners. One of the most popular types is a book review podcast. Often, it will include interviews with authors.

Directions: Download and listen to a podcast about children's books. In your favorite search engine, type in the key words *children's book podcast*. Then, write and rehearse a two-minute review of your chosen podcast. In it, mention the following details:

- the name of the podcast
- the host's name
- special guests
- any sponsors who might help pay for this podcast
- who will enjoy this podcast
- how sounds are used as persuasive techniques in this podcast
- obvious and hidden messages in the podcast
- whether this podcast is healthy or unhealthy

Use the space below for brainstorming and notes.

When you have rehearsed your podcast thoroughly, record it on your computer as a sound file. For information on how to do this, type the words *record a podcast* into your favorite search engine.

Once they are formatted as sound files on your computer, listen to each other's podcasts!

Build a Website

Learn about what goes into website design by building your own! You will need scratch paper, pencils with erasers, and a computer. You will be designing a website on paper with the option of building it on the computer.

Directions:

1. Decide how many pages you want your website to be. You will need a home page and at least one other page. On scratch paper, sketch a design for your website pages. Decide whether you will include advertisements and photos. You may want to assign different people in your group to different pages of the site.

2. Write the text and sketch illustrations for your website, on scratch paper. This is much like creating a magazine layout.

3. You may choose to build this website on a computer. There are several websites that allow you to build a site for free, using a template. In your favorite search engine, type in the key words *free website design*.

4. Follow the computer instructions to build your website on the template given. Type in your text and upload your own digital photos and scanned original artwork. Note that it is illegal to upload someone else's writing and images from the Internet.

5. Give your friends and family the link to your website so that they may enjoy it, too!

6. Finally, deconstruct your website by answering the questions below.

    a. To what age group, economic group, and gender does this website appeal?

    _____

    b. What lifestyle is presented? How is it glamorized?

    _____

    _____

    c. What obvious messages exist on your website?

    _____

    d. What hidden messages exist on your website?

    _____

    e. How is your website an example of healthy or unhealthy media?

    _____

    _____

    _____

Final Project

Congratulations! You have come to the end of *Media Literacy*. To demonstrate your understanding of this subject, you will be creating a final project and deconstructing it.

Directions: Choose a final project to create from the list below. Once you have created it, you need to deconstruct it by writing a short essay describing your media creation.

Forms of Media

- billboard
- front page of magazine/newspaper
- package
- painting
- photograph
- print ad
- radio ad
- recorded song
- sculpture
- television commercial
- website

In your essay, make sure to answer the questions you've used to deconstruct previous forms of media.

This is to certify that

_____

has become a media-literate consumer, skilled in the analysis of:

- Advertisements
- Art
- Magazines
- Movies
- Music
- Newspapers

- Packaging
- Product Placement
- Radio
- Television
- Videogames
- Websites

Signed this _____ of _____ .

_____
Teacher's Signature

Answer Key

Page 10 — How Much Media?

Students chart media consumption to the best of their ability.

Page 11 — How Media Affects You

Grade for effort and depth of thought.

Page 14 — Persuasion in Action

Grade for effort and demonstration of persuasive advertising techniques.

Page 15 — Propaganda

1. This poster sells the idea of saving scrap items.

2. The persuasive advertising techniques include hyperbole, symbols, and bribery.

3. This poster promises that if you save scrap items, the United States will achieve victory in World War II.

4. Answers will vary.

Page 17 — Creating Propaganda

Students deconstruct a form of propaganda to the best of their ability.

Page 18 — Stereotypes

1. Asian people are stereotyped as studious, while Anglos and Latinos are stereotyped as social and fun-loving. All people might be hurt by these stereotypes.

2. Both women are stereotyped. Women might be hurt by this stereotype that says that thin, beautiful women in revealing clothes are popular, while average-looking people in non-revealing clothes are alone.

3. The Native American is stereotyped. Native Americans might be hurt by this unflattering stereotype. Other people might be hurt in assuming this stereotype, as well.

Page 19 — Stereotypes (*cont.*)

Grade for effort and understanding of stereotypes.

Page 20 — Healthy Media?

School meal poster

1. This poster tries to sell the idea that a good lunch includes a hot dish of meat and vegetables, a sandwich, fruit, and milk.

2. This media is healthy because it advocates a nutritious meal.

Soda advertisement

1. This ad is trying to sell soda.

2. Techniques of persuasion include hyperbole, humor, the big lie, warm and fuzzy.

3. This ad is unhealthy because soda is not healthy for consumers.

Page 22 — Healthy Media? *(cont.)*

Students should produce a well-thought-out design for their media and be able to explain why they included the elements they did.

Page 23 — Hidden Messages

1. The obvious message is that we should eat this cereal. The hidden message is that it will give you superpowers that allow you to fly.
2. The obvious messages is that we should eat fruits and vegetables. The hidden message is that if we do, we'll become doctors.
3. The obvious message is that you should keep your cat inside. The hidden message is that an outdoor cat will kill birds.

Page 24 — First Media

Students should have explained what the creators of Newspaper Rock were communicating, to the best of their abilities.

Page 25 — Understanding Petroglyphs

Grade for effort and understanding of petroglyphs.

Page 26 — Make Your Own Petroglyph

Grade for effort and understanding of symbolism.

Page 27 — Print Advertisements

1. This ad is trying to sell Louisville Slugger baseball bats.
2. The company that paid for this ad is called Hillerich and Bradsby Co, Inc.
3. This ad likely appealed to boys and men who could afford a new bat.
4. The advertiser tries to get people to buy these bats by showing photos of the all-stars and noting that they all use this type of bat.
5. The obvious message in this ad is that you should buy a Louisville Slugger bat.
6. After viewing this ad, people may believe that if they buy a Louisville Slugger Bat, they will become an all-star baseball player, too.
7. Answers will vary.

Page 29 — Early Print Ads

1. d
2. c
3. c
4. c
5. a
6. b

Page 31 — Early Print Ads *(cont.)*

1. The Colonel Wm. F. Cody (Buffalo Bill) Historical Picture Co paid for this advertisement.

2. This advertiser is trying to sell exhibitors on the idea of paying for exhibits to accompany this film, and is also trying to persuade people to put up posters.

3. You might have found almost any type of person at this film—both genders and any age, as long as they had the expendable income to pay for a ticket.

4. Three persuasive phrases that advertisers use to get potential consumers' attention include: "has attracted the attention of the entire world," "five-reel thriller that will live forever," and "the posters will stop the crowds."

5. In contemporary times, Buffalo Bill's war against the Native Americans is seen as politically-incorrect at best, and genocide at worst. Unless Native Americans were championed in this film, no exhibitor would want to be a part of this project today.

Page 33 — Contemporary Print Ads

Grade students for their efforts and understanding of contemporary print advertisements.

Pages 34 and 35 — Compare and Contrast

Grade students for their efforts and understanding of advertisements, how they have changed over time, and clarity of the Venn diagram.

Page 36 — Create Your Own Print Ad

Grade for effort and understanding of components in a print advertisement.

Page 38 — Early Billboards

1. f
2. d
3. e
4. c
5. b
6. a

Page 39 — Early Billboards *(cont.)*

1. Gerald Ford Jr. hoped to win the position of United States representative.

2. Answers may vary—grade for understanding and effort.

3. This billboard would appeal to Republican voters who want a young representative working for them.

4. The "you" in the slogan, "to work for you in Congress" is public constituents.

5. There is a circle of stars in the upper left corner of this billboard to mimic the stars on the American flag.

Pages 40 and 41 — Today's Billboards

Grade for effort and understanding of billboard advertisements.

Pages 42 and 43 — Compare and Contrast

Grade students for their efforts and understanding of billboards, how they have changed over time, and clarity of the Venn diagram.

Page 44 — Create a Billboard

Grade for effort and understanding of billboard components.

Page 46 — Radio Ad Techniques

Answers will vary, below are possible answers.

1. Have people speak in sultry, cultured voices, possibly with British accents.

2. Have many people talking or cheering at once.

3. Use foreboding music, eerie voices, sounds of squeaking doors and glass shattering.

4. Kittens mewing, puppies yapping, cute children's voices, lullabies and nursery rhymes, lambs or other baby animals calling.

5. Patriotic music, recognizable tunes like Richard Wagner's "Bridal Chorus," alarm clocks roosters crowing to symbolize morning, crickets to symbolize night, etc.

6. Particularly high- or low-pitched voices, yodeling, tongue-twisters, funny squeaks or slide-whistles, goats bleating, etc.

7. Serious, business-like voices or earnest friendly voices, enthusiastic voices lauding a product.

8. A word, phrase, or sound repeated over and over—like a jingle.

9. A voice that sounds scientific, the noise of scientific machinery in the background, facts and statistics read on the air, machinery noises.

Page 47 — Historic Radio Ads

Grade for effort and understanding of radio advertisements from the past.

Page 48 — Contemporary Radio Ads

Grade for effort and understanding of contemporary radio advertisements.

Page 49 — Your Radio Commercial

Grade for effort and understanding of how to write and record a radio advertisement.

Pages 50 and 51 — The First Radio Shows

Grade for effort and understanding of chosen radio show.

Answer Key *(cont.)*

Page 52 —War of the Worlds

1. A narrator introduces the story, and then a radio newscast begins. Music plays, and is abruptly interrupted by the announcer saying that Martians have landed on Earth.

2. People who didn't catch the introduction to this radio piece, and who tuned in only to the simulated broadcast with its reports of Martians landing and scientists confirming this, truly believed Martians had landed on Earth.

3. This is open to students' interpretation. Look for reasonable, thoughtful answers.

Page 53 — Children's Radio Shows

Grade for effort and understanding of children's radio shows.

Page 54 — Create Your Radio Show

Grade for effort and understanding of how to write and record a radio show.

Page 57 — Classic TV Commercials

Grade for effort and understanding of television commercials from the past.

Page 58 — Today's TV Commercials

Grade for effort and understanding of contemporary television commercials.

Page 59 — Compare and Contrast

Grade students for effort and understanding of how television commercials have changed over time, and clarity of their Venn diagrams.

Page 60 — Create Your Commercial

Grade for effort and understanding of how to write and record a television commercial.

Page 61 — Your Television Journal

Grade journal for effort and thoughtfulness.

Page 62 — News on Television

Grade for effort and understanding of lead news stories.

Page 63 — Healthy TV News?

Grade for effort and understanding of how particular news stories affect the viewer.

Page 64 — The Role of Sponsors

Grade for effort and understanding of the role of television sponsors.

Page 65 — Messages in Television

Grade for effort and understanding of hidden and obvious messages in television.

Page 66 — Turning Off Your TV

Grade for effort and understanding of this particular website.

Page 67 — Alternatives to Television

Grade for effort and creativity.

Answer Key *(cont.)*

Page 68 — TV–Turnoff Week Journal

Grade for effort and depth of thought.

Page 69 — Music

Grade for effort and depth of thought.

Page 70 — Controversy in Music

1. A listener would benefit from file sharing by getting free music and having an online community with which to chat about music. However, someone downloading music for free might have to pay a hefty penalty, and might even go to jail.

2. A musician would benefit from people file sharing music because of increased exposure and publicity. The musician would be harmed by decreased music sales.

3. Grade student compositions for effort and understanding of one controversial issue as it relates to music.

Page 71 — Analyze a Song

Grade for effort and understanding of chosen song.

Page 72 — Music Videos

1. People that like foreboding, darkly romantic music and gothic images and stories.

2. Techniques of persuasion in this video are fear and symbols.

3. One lifestyle in this video is poor and destitute. The other is rough and gothic. The latter is more glamorous, due to the all-black clothes and facial expressions and spider tattoo.

4. The obvious message in this video is not to wander off without the speaker or forget him/her. The little lost boys reinforce that message by getting lost in the middle of a thunderstorm.

5. The hidden message in this video is open to students' interpretation. They may suggest that children should not go off into the forest alone, or that we should help poor people so that they aren't starving. Some may interpret the band as sinister and threatening to potential friends/partners.

Page 73 — Music Videos *(cont.)*

Grade for effort and understanding of music videos.

Page 74 — Make a Music Video

Grade for effort and understanding of how to write and create a music video.

Page 75 — Videogames

Grade for effort and understanding of how videogame consoles have changed over time, and for thoughtfulness in student's analysis of own videogame habits.

Page 76 — Videogame Ads

Grade for effort and understanding of components of videogame print advertisement.

Page 77 — Videogame Ads *(cont.)*

Grade for effort and understanding of how to deconstruct a videogame print advertisement.

Page 78 — Violence in Videogames

Grade for effort and understanding of favorite videogame, as well as how violence may appear in this game.

Answer Key *(cont.)*

Page 79 — Physical Effects

Grade for effort and depth of thought regarding physical effects of playing videogames.

Page 80 — Your Favorite Videogame

Grade for effort and depth of thought regarding student's favorite videogame.

Page 81 — Videogame Debate

Grade each student team for effort, as well as for depth of thought in formulating and presenting arguments.

Page 83 — Packages of the Past

1. This package was paid for by F.W. Thayer.
2. This package would appeal to people who are ill.
3. The obvious message of this package is to eat these for coughs, colds, and hoarseness.
4. The hidden message of this package is you'll be as strong as a unicorn.
5. The lifestyle on this package shows a battle scene with a glamorous unicorn overcoming a lion.

Page 84 — Packages of Today

Grade for effort and understanding of how to deconstruct a contemporary package.

Page 85 — Color, Shape, and Text

1. blue
2. something unusual like a hexagon or a cone
3. green
4. purple
5. a cartoon character or animal
6. red
7. Information about both the movie and the character's particular role—information that isn't included in the movie so that buyers feel like they are "in the know."

Page 86 — Compare and Contrast

Label One

1. The product is horehound balsam. The brand name is "Keatings."
2. Students may note that the vertical writing on either side of the photo stands out. They may note the different fonts, or the enlarged font size at the top of the page.
3. The image on this label stands out because the child is smiling and holding the bottle. For students, it may stand out because of the dated image, as well.
4. This label promises buyers a sure cure of coughs, colds, sore throats, and hoarseness.
5. The slogan is "Small Doses, Sure Cure."

Label Two

6. This product is cold and pain relief medicine. The brand name is Goodheart's.
7. Students may note the different fonts, sizes, heart-shaped bullets, and underlined word.
8. Students may note that the heart logo stands out on this label.

Page 86 — Compare and Contrast *(cont.)*

9. This package label promise buyers instant relief of sore throat, headache, cough, and fever.

10. This package uses the slogan, "feel the love with Goodhearts."

11. Grade for effort and understanding of how packages have changed from the past to the present day.

Page 88 — Design Your Own Package

Grade for effort and student understanding of package design.

Page 90 — Product Placement Methods

Grade for effort and student attempts to spot product placement in a movie trailer.

Page 91 — Products in Books

1. Candy bars are used as counting tools.

2. Students will likely note that the candy bar manufacturer paid for the product to appear in the book. Some may consider whether the publisher paid for the privilege of featuring this candy bar, however.

3. Children who are just learning to count will enjoy this book—ages 2–5.

4. Readers will learn to count.

5. Readers may learn to love and desire candy bars. They may learn to see chocolate as linked with education.

6. Some students may say that this media is healthy because it's educational and fun. Others may say that this media is unhealthy because it teaches children to love a brand-name fattening product in the guise of a counting book.

Page 92 — Products in Videogames

1. Advertisers want to put their products in video games so that players will see and buy these products.

2. Videogame designers agree to feature name-brand products in their games because they are paid, and/or because it gives the games a more realistic quality.

3. Students will have varying views. Some may like product placement in video games because they enjoy the product or agree that it gives a game a more realistic quality. Others may feel that advertisers are force-feeding them messages to buy a brand-name product.

4. Students' answers will vary. Some may say that people play video games without even noticing product placement. Others will note that subconsciously, players see and desire these products. Students may note that players deliberately buy products featured in video games, believing the items to be part of a desirable lifestyle.

5. Videogame Scene—Grade students for effort and understanding of videogame product placement.

Page 93 — Products on Television

Grade for effort and student attempts to locate product placement in a television program.

Page 94 — Taste-Test

Grade students for effort, understanding, and conduct.

Page 95 — Products in Movies

Grade for effort and student attempts to locate product placement in a movie.

Page 96 — Magazines

1. This magazine is called *Leslie's Weekly.*

2. This magazine appealed to men of legal age.

3. The Spanish-American War was taking place.

4. This magazine cover sends an obvious message to readers to help their country.

5. The hidden message of this cover is that you will be a noble patriot if you help your country in time of war.

6. The flag on the cover symbolizes patriotism.

7. The bugle on this cover symbolizes a call to action.

Page 98 — Tricks in Photography *(cont.)*

Answers are open to student interpretation.

Page 99 — Magazines for Children

Grade for effort and depth of analysis regarding magazines.

Page 100 — Messages in Magazines

1. Students may note that the beautiful kids stand out on this cover, along with flashy graphics and fonts.

2. The obvious message on this cover is that being attractive is important for happiness and popularity.

3. Students may see hidden messages including one that says thin is beautiful, that only thin and beautiful people find boy/girlfriends, that sexiness is critical, and looks and popularity are of vast importance.

4. Students may point out that this media is healthy because it teaches you how to dress in the latest fashions and be popular. More likely, they'll point out that the focus on image and clothing is shallow and can contribute to insecurity and eating disorders.

Page 101 — Messages in Magazines *(cont.)*

1. Students may point out the intrigue of kids planting a garden, along with the commanding title and interesting headlines. They may note that the kids on the cover don't look like supermodels.

2. The obvious message is that life is interesting, and full of fun and helpful things to do.

3. Students may find hidden messages telling them that service to others is important, that spending time in nature is desirable, and that students have a responsibility to help the earth.

4. Students may say that this media is unhealthy because it asks them to help address global warming and become stewards of the earth. Most will likely say that this is a healthy form of media because of its suggestions for wholesome activities.

Page 102 — Your Favorite Magazine

Grade for effort and depth of analysis of student's favorite magazine.

Page 103 — Design a Magazine

Grade for effort and student understanding of what constitutes a healthy magazine.

Pages 105 and 106 — Front Pages of the Past

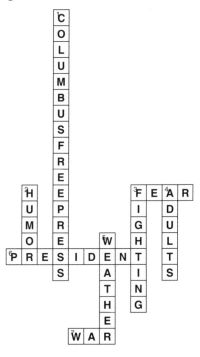

Page 107 — Front Pages of Today

Grade for effort and student understanding of contemporary newspaper front page.

Page 108 — Your Local Paper

Grade for effort and student analysis of local paper.

Page 109 — The Op/Ed Section

Grade for effort and understanding of the Op-Ed section of student's local paper.

Page 110 — A Letter to the Editor

Grade for effort, readability, and clarity of opinion.

Page 111 — A Letter to the Editor *(cont)*

Grade for effort and understanding of how to submit a letter to a local paper.

Page 112 — Spinning a Story

Grade for effort and understanding of angles and how they are used in three stories covering the same topic.

Page 113 — Spinning a Story *(cont.)*

Grade for effort and depth of thought in comparing and contrasting three newspaper articles.

Answer Key *(cont.)*

Page 114 — Art

1. Millions of families and individuals across the country lost their jobs and homes. They became homeless and destitute, in some cases starving.

2. The Farm Security Administration paid for this media.

3. Students may note that this art appeals to adults in general, and mothers in particular—most specifically possibly to poor mothers. They might note that this piece appeals to those most affected by the Depression.

4. The lifestyle presented is one of poverty. It is not glamorized.

5. The obvious message that exists are that the Depression has made young mothers homeless and poverty-stricken.

6. Students may note that hidden messages urge us to help these homeless people, or that we should feel guilty for having a home and enough to eat.

Page 115 — Painting

1. In this painting, the United States and Great Britain signed a peace treaty in Ghent, Belgium on December 24, 1814.

2. Students may notice the flags that symbolize the U.S. and Great Britain, along with the white flag that symbolizes surrender, and the warriors—one symbolizing each country—holding hands as they descend the stairs. A peace dove flies at the top of the painting.

3. The obvious message of this painting is that symbols of the U.S. and Britain have joined together.

4. Students may speculate that the hidden message is one of peace and prosperity, inspired by the dove and the lush columns and velvet curtains.

5. The lifestyle is sumptuous and regal, glamorized by elaborate costumes, columns, and curtains.

6. Student opinions will differ. Some will say that this is a healthy form of media because it represents peace between previously warring nations.

Page 117 — Sculpture

1. This sculpture was created by Daniel Chester French, and it is located in the Lincoln Memorial in Washington, D.C.

2. Many types of people would enjoy this sculpture, but mostly history buffs and people who love this particular president.

3. Lincoln went to war against Southern secessionists in a protest against both secessionism and slavery. He was assassinated by John Wilkes Booth.

4. Abraham Lincoln is portrayed as a capable, controlled man who is important enough to deserve a sculpture of this magnitude.

5. Students may see Lincoln's pensive expression as a hidden message of his grave concerns for the country. They may also read into his expression a foreshadow of his assassination.

6. Students may point out that those Southerners who still favor secessionism might find this sculpture offensive.

Page 118 — Sculpture (cont.)

Grade students own sculptures for effort and understanding of sculpture and symbolism.

Page 119 — Photography

1. The United States sent Japanese Americans to internment camps after the bombing of Pearl Harbor during World War II. The Japanese Americans had to leave their homes, schools, and work places. They were forced to live in these camps.

2. Students may speculate that Japanese Americans are waiting in line with their belongings to board a bus to the internment camp.

3. The obvious message in this photo is that the subjects are relocating.

4. The hidden messages might be that the little boy is worried about the little girl, or more deeply, that the U.S. should not have interned Japanese Americans because it was cruel to displace them.

5. Student answers will vary.

6. Student answers will vary. Some may feel that this is a healthy example of media because it depicts an era in history that all should know about. Others may find it an unhealthy example of media because it "reopens old wounds" or creates feelings of hostility, shame, or anger among Japanese Americans.

Grade for effort and student understanding of photography as media.

Page 120 — Comic Books

1. This comic book is likely about nuclear energy.

2. The book appeals to young readers with an animated atom and a young man on the cover, as well as with kid-friendly font.

3. The U.S. dropped a nuclear bomb on Hiroshima.

4. Students may speculate that GE put out this book to gather support for, and understanding of, nuclear energy. Some may observe that this comic book is propaganda that tries to defend the bomb dropped on Hiroshima.

5. Open to student interpretation.

Page 121 — Comic Books *(cont.)*

Grade for effort and depth of thought about comic books from the United States and Japan.

Page 122 — Graffiti Versus Murals

Grade for effort and depth of thought about the differences between graffiti and murals.

Answer Key *(cont.)*

Page 123 — Create a Mural

Grade for effort and understanding of what constitutes a mural.

Page 124 — Websites

1. Kids in junior high will enjoy this web page.

2. There are at least three news stories on this web page.

3. There are at least three advertisements on this web page.

4. Students may observe that this photo was chosen because the girl is attractive and has a diamond ring which is a symbol of wealth and beauty.

5. Students may say that this web page is healthy because it offers news—especially a reminder to hug your mom. They may find that it is unhealthy because it has so many advertisements, and a focus on the idea that thin and beautiful is most desirable.

Page 125 — Popular Home Pages

Grade for effort and depth of analysis of one home page.

Page 126 — Websites for Young People

Grade for effort and depth of analysis of one home page and how it appeals to young people.

Page 127 — Author Websites

Grade for effort and depth of analysis of one author's home page and healthy or unhealthy messages.

Page 128 — Podcasts

Grade for effort and understanding of both how to create, and how to analyze, a podcast.

Page 129 — Build a Website

Grade for effort and understanding of how to create and build a website.

Page 130 — Final Project

Grade final project for effort, and for a demonstration of components of media literacy as covered in this book.